The author is a singer-songwriter, poet, radio-TV presenter, actor and voice-over artist who descended into the abyss of crime, violence and drug addiction, but found the strength, courage and support to ascend in life. Enriched by these experiences, the author now seeks to empower those grappling with such challenges and to steer others clear from the mental and physical prison of torture, pain, anger, regret, remorse, resistance, guilt and shame.

This book is dedicated, firstly, to our beloved and beautiful Mama Jean. She loved music without frontiers. She liked every kind of Caribbean music, along with Blues, Soul, Country, Gospel, Latin, Jazz, Classical and Vintage Rock 'n' Roll. Above all, she loved life, people and dance. Two of her favourite records were: 'It Takes Two' by Marvin Gaye and Tammi Terrell, which was played over and over again, to my delight. The other was 'Three Steps to Heaven' by Eddie Cochran, a charming slice of teen beat rock 'n' roll, but the lad didn't know one thing: in rehab, there are twelve steps to Heaven.

To Mamie, my maternal grandmother and spiritual guide; and to our beloved sister Verina who recently departed from this world, and last, but not least, to all suffering and recovering drug and alcohol addicts and their families, throughout the world.

Tamara Gabriel

FROM REHAB TO LIFE

AUSTIN MACAULEY PUBLISHERS™

LONDON • CAMBRIDGE • NEW YORK • SHARJAH

A CIP catalogue record for this title is available from the British Library.

ISBN 9781786297624 (Paperback)
ISBN 9781786297631 (Hardback)
ISBN 9781528951920 (ePub e-book)

www.austinmacauley.com

First Published (2020)
Austin Macauley Publishers Ltd
25 Canada Square
Canary Wharf
London
E14 5LQ

My endless thanks to Clive Anderson, for his vision and positive support; and for proofreading my number of submissions.

A big thank you also to Global City Productions for their invaluable support.

Thank you, Ray Hayden, for creating the beautiful cover graphics; and to all of the staff and my peers whom I met in rehab and in the Fellowships of NA and AA, and to everyone I worked with in writing this book and for bringing the project to a successful completion. Many thanks to all of my family and friends, for their support, and to Connor Browne, Vinh Tran, Samantha Hughes and everyone at Austin Macauley for making this publication possible.

My thanks, lastly and most importantly, to Almighty God, for giving me the strength and vision to be able to take my negative experiences and turn them into a positive motivation that I can now share with the world.

"Thank You, God."

Contents

Chapter 1

Paradise Lost

I was born Vander Christian Algernon Pierre, on the volcanic, mountainous and gloriously green Windward Island of Dominica. Enriched with 366 rivers, it attracts naturalists and the yachting fraternity with its breath-taking beauty.

My father, Rupert Martin Pierre, nicknamed Bogart, was reputedly a notorious, handsome and natty dresser, and leader of a steel band that toured the Caribbean. He never mentioned the name of the outfit and I never asked.

My mother, Jean Joseph, now Jean Anderson, was an only child and renowned for her beauty and intelligence. We lived in a large house on the hill of Zikak, overlooking the town of Portsmouth and its harbour, with my younger siblings Glen and Verina. My father is no longer with us on this earth and my mother is bedbound with Alzheimer's and other complications, requiring, and getting 24/7 live-in and loving care.

My journey into this world wasn't straight forward, as the doctor had advised my grandmother, Mamie, and my mother to terminate the pregnancy, as Mama Jean would be barely eighteen years of age on my arrival into the world. There was then the social stigma of being an underage and unmarried mother. No doubt, Mamie's spirituality and her Roman Catholic beliefs, combined with my mother's willingness to endure my nine months' journey into this world, influenced their decision not to abort. The start of my life's journey was in their hands. For Mamie's courageous, supportive and loving care, I am, and shall be, eternally grateful.

I was oblivious to all that was to come, as I admired the elegant yachts dressed in brilliant white, sitting blissfully upon the glistening Caribbean Sea. As I stood on the veranda, with a white mongrel dog playing in the yard, I visualised myself as the yacht's owner or saw myself as one of the older boys who swam out half a mile or more to those dream boats and back to the shore for the fun of it.

My father and mother left us in the loving care of my Mum's mum, whom I've always called Mamie instead of Grandma. They said they were off to seek a better life and would send for us later. My mother told me that I had said I would find her even if I had to walk across the sea, as I stood on the edge of the jetty in Portsmouth Harbour.

Now I understand how my parents' well-intentioned departure left me feeling abandoned, angry and bewildered. After all, we had everything: the big house and hired domestic help. Through the rehab process, I learnt that my addictive personality was triggered by that first sense of abandonment. It left me declaring Mamie my mum, and feeling different from other children, as I sat there with a blank mind. On occasion, I'd escape up to the mountains and live life there. There were times when the moon was so huge and so close, as it hung beneath a star-studded sky, above an orchestra of crickets, that it seemed possible to touch it from the top of a tree.

I remember catching crabs and crayfish in the river opposite our home, and carefully walking through Pappy Jean Pierre's cocoa plantation, watching out for snakes slithering through the cocoa leaves that carpeted the ground. Life was a wonderful adventure. That same spirit of adventure found me racing down the mountain road on a homemade go-kart, for which I received serious grief from Mamie, and an abrupt end to any further expeditions of that sort. Neddy Jo, my friend and elder from next door, got a beating that could be heard a hundred yards away. He never rode a go-kart again. I'm sure such loving and firm parenting saved our lives.

Mamie taught me how to pray long before I could read and write, and I was reading, writing and attending school from the age of three, to the amazement of many. The prayer that stood out most went like this: "This night before I go to sleep, I pray you God my soul to keep. If I should die before I wake, I pray you God my soul to take." I became conscious of man's mortality and not to take life for granted. My stepfather, Clive, told me that it also happens to be Mama Jean's favourite prayer.

Mamie also instilled in me the need to value and respect others of all colours and creeds, and to be compassionate in dealing with mental and physical disabilities. She also taught me to defend myself, by insisting that I leave the house and find the boy who hit me with a stone and return the favour. I wasn't to return until the mission was accomplished; those were her terms, even though the boy was my senior by some years. Shocked by the fact that I didn't receive any kissing and cuddling, I left the house determined to catch the boy. In a matter of minutes, I returned the favour, leaving him in tears. I realised from that moment on that no one was invincible, and we all feel pain, and it's not a nice thing to inflict or receive. I learned about unconditional love, which I received from Mamie, and it didn't include being bullied or being used as a doormat.

My first desire was to be a priest, but that was short-lived, as I soon discovered that Catholic Priests don't get married. Mamie taught me how to sing and as a result, I channelled my energies into joining the church choir as soon as possible.

Receiving parcels from Mama Jean and Daddy Rupert from London, England, was a joyous occasion, as we anticipated what was inside. These parcels ensured that Verina, born after me, Glen and I, received toys, shoes and clothes that most children didn't have. I remember being humbled and grateful for such good fortune.

This wasn't the case when I was told that we were to go to England to join our parents. I was fearful and angry at the idea of leaving Dominica. I couldn't bear the thought of no more churning the coconut ice cream for Miss May, Neddy Jo's mum, for which I would receive half a large cup of the heavenly stuff. And what about my visits to Pappy Jean, who'd call me in his deep loving voice? I'd hurry to his house on the beach, beside the river that ran through his cocoa plantation, from the foot of the mountain to the sea. The fragrance of cocoa beans drying in the sun on banana leaves was a predominant feature at his house, where I drank the sweetest, freshest and most delicious cocoa, boiled in fresh coconut milk, with fresh vanilla pods, cinnamon and nutmeg added.

I thought of Papa Juslin, Mamie's father, who caught lobster when he wasn't cultivating the plot on the mountain. I fondly remember him calling at our home, after his descent from the garden, bringing yams, sweet potatoes and dasheen, which he'd harvested to share with Mamie.

His passing brought peace and relief, as well as pain, having watched him cling to life with every breath, for what seemed an eternity. I didn't see Mamie cry, but I felt her grief. I was angry with Papa Juslin's wife, who'd deserted him at his moment of greatest need; but luckily, Mamie was there to cater to those needs. Without anger or resentment, she cleaned and fed my great-grandfather, who was tall and athletically built, with blonde hair and blue eyes. Ma Da, my great-grandmother and Papa Juslin's first wife, had passed away some months before I was born; she was a beautiful, tough and loving Indian woman for whom I felt considerable affection, although we had never met.

Mamie, known to others as Miss Ina Valerie, was always boiling different herbs and buying medicine for our little brother Glen, who was regularly ill, as he tended to eat the Dominican soil. I could never understand where he got an appetite for that stuff. On top of all that, Mamie was a first-class seamstress, designer, cutter and fitter of women's clothes, who taught sewing at school and manufactured clothes for the Portsmouth Department Store as well as for individuals. Occasionally, I ran errands to collect money as well as delivered the odd outfit on Mamie's behalf.

I hadn't learnt to swim despite my ambition to reach those yachts anchored half a mile or so offshore. I hadn't even climbed to the summit of that mountain, at the foot of which stood our new home in Lagoon, now that Mamie had moved from Zikak to be close to Pappy Jean's place. I wanted to bathe in that river further up the mountain and discover those big frogs they call mountain chicken, because of their flavour. I wanted to see what other wildlife was up there.

I continued to play with Neddy Jo and my cousins Lennox and Aaron, who were also neighbours, and having kindled a secret but loving relationship with my fair-skinned cousin Aerolene, there was no way I was leaving the island. And what about those Sunday baths with Mamie, at the estuary of another river, further away in Tatan? Mamie said that was the best place to bathe, where the river met the sea.

I was living the life of a prince, with a maid to escort me to school, and I trusted that they'd forgive me for peeping at them when they went to the loo or the shower. I was in love with my natural surroundings. I'd transcend to the moon at nights to meet the man with a bundle of firewood on his back. I captained those coconut-shy boats that I put out to sea, wondering whose beach we'd eventually land at. I enjoyed these flights of fantasy. They seemed to enhance the beauty of this world and create a better one, even though I was already living a privileged life. Was this an early sign of my addictive personality? I became defiant, rebellious and angry about leaving home. I didn't want to see the snow like other children and adults, and deep down, I didn't feel that life could or would be any better than what I was enjoying.

My anger and defiance turned into sadness and then humility, as I realised and accepted my powerlessness in the situation while we criss-crossed the island, bidding farewell to family and friends. I was fearful of the narrow mountain roads with their sheer drops and wondered why we didn't avoid such danger and travel by sea. When we arrived in London, I was instantly shocked by the lack of colour in clothing, cars, houses and flying birds. I asked why there were so many factories with curtains and was surprised to learn that they were family homes. I'd never seen houses stuck together before, and any building with a chimney was a factory where I came from. The underground freaked me out as we travelled from Victoria Station, with windows that looked out into darkness.

When we arrived in Hackney E9, I asked my mum where were the maids? I listened in disbelief as she said that there were no maids in the house. Feeling like a stranger in my new surroundings, I wondered who was doing all the cooking and cleaning. The answer came some days later when I was given a knife and taught to peel potatoes by my mum, who insisted that I call her Jean, the same applied to Verina and Glen. My two sisters, Heather and Sandra, who were born in London, were the only ones allowed to call her mum. That arrangement hurt me deeply as I felt that I was living in a two-tier system, with an invisible barrier that separated me from the Caribbean, from my two youngest sisters and my parents.

We all called our dad, dad. He wasn't going to be called by his name by any of his children. Sandra was still in nappies. Apart from learning to peel and cook potatoes at the age of seven, I was given routine chores that included shopping, sweeping, hoovering, cleaning, washing up, bottle making, nappy changing and laundering at the local laundrette in the absence of a washing machine.

This wasn't the wonderful family reunion I expected. Admittedly, we were one of the few families that owned our house, while most people we knew lived in rooms that were sometimes partitioned to create an illusion of two rooms, divided by a curtain. My mother was beautiful, and my father was handsome and built like an ox. In all honesty, I felt like an intruder and an outsider in this new and bigger family environment, which also included tenants in the building. My roots were in Dominica and here I was, in London, England, trying to bond with my parents and two other sisters, amid daily chores that seemed to rob me of my childhood, in terms of playing with other children or studying books at my leisure. My anger and resentment at my situation was fuelled by the pain of being uprooted from Dominica.

Chapter 2

Shades of the Prison House

I believed my parents were crazy for coming to England, as we had no maids here, which resulted in the allocation of so many chores to me. I felt as if I'd descended from heaven into hell. My standard of living hadn't improved, in fact, quite the contrary.

As if that wasn't enough, along came the savage beatings I suffered daily at the hands of my deranged father. Furthermore, we all witnessed the ugly, heated arguments and violence that our father launched against our mum. I began to wonder whether they were my true parents, because I felt as if I was living on the wrong planet with the wrong people. I was riddled with constant fear for myself and my mother, who'd say to me that the longest rope has an end, whenever I'd ask her why didn't she leave my father. Suddenly, I saw my childhood as a prison sentence with a release date too far away to contemplate.

One morning, as we stood in the sunshine in our back garden, in a moment's reprieve from all the madness, I told my mother I'd buy her a house by the river one day. I loved my mother dearly and was too young to understand and appreciate that I was helping a young mother maintain a family home as well as fulfil her ambitions to improve her skills and better all our lives.

Somehow, I managed to do very well at school, I always looked forward to attending it and learning, but was reluctant to leave at the final bell. I began to envy those who looked forward to going home at four p.m., wishing I were one of them, with parents like theirs. I had a hernia operation at eleven or twelve years of age due to the heavy labour that was included in my domestic chores. Our family physician, Dr Murphy, questioned my condition as he prescribed nerve tablets for a child of nine years, who was still wetting the bed and getting beaten for it. I was too frightened and ashamed to tell him the truth. Retrospectively, I feel such conditions fed the disease of addiction in me.

There's a catalogue of woeful tales I could go into, but I choose not to, as that would be another book by itself. I also found racism insane as my grandmother was almost white and my great-grandfather, Papa Juslin, had blonde hair and blue eyes and it went totally against my upbringing. Although my father's side of the family was black, I never heard him pass a racist remark.

I now understand that I'm as sick as my secrets. Keeping the violence and fear of my father a secret, together with racist wars in and out of school, and being robbed of my childhood, with the burden of so many responsibilities so early in life, made me sick and prepared me for a life addicted to drugs, alcohol and crime. I know that others have had similar experiences without taking that route, but I did.

My father changed our surname from Pierre to Peter, on advice from my old-fashioned headmistress at St John The Baptist School in Hackney. She reminded me of a character you'd find in one of those old films about the British Empire when she told my father that the English equivalent was more appropriate, now that we were in England.

Amid all the gloom, there were fleeting yet wonderful moments of really unforgettable joy, especially the regular house parties that my parents held. I would get a drop of Teacher's whisky, topped up with dilute-to-taste orange juice, and I learned a lot of slick dance moves from my father's dapper friends: Denzil, Wendy and Saga. I watched them dance to the sounds of 'Rude Boys Don't Fear', 'Train to Skaville', 'The Whip', and soul classics like 'Do You Like Good Music' by Arthur Conley and 'You Don't Know Like I Know' by Sam and Dave.

One spiritual concern followed another. I served as an acolyte in our local church and was also a member of the choir at St John The Baptist Church on King Edward Road, Hackney. I won my first singing competition at the Church Boys' Guild, at the age of seven, the Guild being run by the nuns in St Joseph's Hospice, next door to the morgue on Mare Street.

Having heard how, during an English Literature class, I'd spontaneously turned a poem into a song and sang it really well, a local band called Trax invited me to join them as lead singer. They were teenagers on the verge of leaving our school, Cardinal Pole, and despite being just twelve years old, I gladly accepted. The poem was entitled 'The Queen of Hearts', and I'm grateful to its creator, for the opportunity it afforded me. We held our first full rehearsal in Clapton, Hackney, in St Jude's Church Hall, Blurton Road, off Chatsworth Road Market, and this Sunday afternoon meeting went on to become a regular feature. We were the supporting act to Glenroy Oakley and the Oracles; later renamed Greyhound, when they had a hit with a cover version of 'Moon River'. Glenroy said I had a good voice and suggested that I attended some voice coaching, in order to take it to a higher level. Although I felt insulted at the suggestion, I soon realised that he meant well, and that I had to be willing to learn. After all, I was only twelve. The soul band was a tight outfit and Glenroy's singing was flawless.

Mamie designed and tailored silk and satin shirts for my performances. I always gave my parents every penny earned from each performance. I loved escaping in song on stage, or anywhere else for that matter. It gave me the strength to endure the dark side of my childhood.

My parents had now bought a second house at 7 Groombridge Road Hackney and let out our first house at 14 Banbury Road. Our new garden at Groombridge Road ran into Well Street Common, which made it a little easier to slip out and play cricket and football, and to enjoy bike races along the paths, with mostly older boys.

I escaped living in fear of my father and alleviated some of the pain, anger and frustration at losing the joys of childhood in domestic drudgery by writing poetry, reading books and learning to play a guitar. I also escaped by becoming an all-round sportsman who was especially addicted to long-distance and cross-country running, as my troubles disappeared with every mile. I became Hackney School's boxing champion and represented Cardinal Pole in football, cricket and athletics, specializing in the 400 metres and shot putting. I also represented the school in gymnastics and cross-country events in the wet and cold of winter at Parliament Hill.

I remember the shame and embarrassment of keeping my back to the wall in the changing room, to hide the lash scars: a result of vicious beatings inflicted by my father, using a doubled-up rope, his heaviest belt or electric flex-wire, for the slightest infraction or even for nothing at all. These assaults were sometimes carried out behind locked doors to prevent my mother from intervening or me from fleeing.

As I grew older and bigger, I nevertheless enjoyed myself as much as I could, when I could, with my friends, girls and boys alike, none of whom were welcome at our door. I took refuge and comfort in moments of kissing, cuddling and holding hands with my schoolgirl sweethearts and female fans. Writing and receiving love letters in and out of classes, meeting at the school dance and going to the pictures with my girlfriends, felt like I was floating on a cloud. I enjoyed the female adulation and male respect I received before, during and after my stage performances. I felt like a mega star in the making with girls chasing me down the streets, and once resorted to hiding in a shop doorway, hoping they'd pass me by, all to no avail. As for being on stage, it was like being in heaven, where all my troubles vanished in an instant.

I was heartbroken when my parents' refusal to give me the money needed to buy a 100 watts Marshall PA system forced me to quit the band, just as we had started playing bigger and better venues. I'd given my parents thousands of pounds, which I thought was being saved on my behalf, and didn't dare ask what had become of it all. I felt betrayed, when even a pair of Levi's was denied me.

I asked for a brand-new bike and got a second-hand one instead. I asked for a guitar for Christmas and received a plastic one instead of a wooden one. On that plastic guitar, I taught myself to play some Beatles songs until Sandra, the youngest family member, broke it. It was never replaced, and its loss was both painful and infuriating. As for that second-hand bike, the fork snapped as I slowed to a halt, approaching the garden door on Well Street Common. I thanked God that I wasn't speeding on the Common at the time and vowed that I would buy myself the very best of everything when I left home. Did I set myself up for a life of crime with that statement? Who knows! In spite of all this, I loved my violent father and my beautiful and intelligent mother, who was very careful with the purse strings. I understood that there were five of us to cater for but felt that I deserved the occasional thing I needed or wanted from my own money.

Mum did very well in her job as a secretary and later on as a model, dancer and actress. She appeared in the Bond movie 'On Her Majesty's Secret Service', in a theatrical production of 'Hair' and in 'The Chicago Trial Conspiracy', a BBC Two drama. She'd talk about Fred Zinnemann, the film director, and other big names who had offered her work. I was so proud of my mum and greatly admired her irrepressible nature. Even though my father tried to sabotage her chances, by burning her typewriter and her modelling portfolio, she kept bouncing right back.

I thank her with all my heart, for the many times that she'd intervened, when beatings were inflicted upon me by my father. As a result, there were occasions when she'd find herself on the receiving end of them as well. Her aspirin overdoses necessitated hospital stays, while her hand-through-a-glass-door-panel resulted in an injury that required hospital attention and stitches. Over the years, she'd left the family on many occasions to escape from my father but had always returned. She was a powerful woman, who, in our hellhole, was determined to raise her children as best as she could.

To outsiders, we appeared a middleclass family, living the life in a big house. Mum was beautiful and looked so remarkably young that when I was thirteen or fourteen years of age, people often thought I was her boyfriend. The fanciful longings of schoolboys, including my friends, used to upset me.

My dad was a hard-working nightshift worker, to give credit where it's due, employed at Ford's, Dagenham. Family and friends, who knew about the beatings he administered, remained silent, fearing him and his notorious reputation back home. Mamie never feared my father and would tell him to stop the violence. She even advised me to call the police, but I never did. A friend of his once confided to me that dad was reputed to be the baddest man in Dominica in his day, yet to his friends he was a generous man and would willingly give what I'd ask of him, provided my mother approved. He'd wanted me to join him at Ford's or to join the Army or Air force to learn a trade, whereas mum wanted me to attend university, where I dearly wanted to study Law and fulfil an aspiration of becoming a Perry Mason-type lawyer.

At school, I was in the top class of the academic stream and would usually finish in the top five in most subjects, excelling in English Language and Literature, History, Economics, Geography, Religious Knowledge, Natural Science, French and German. How I did so well, even in my weaker subjects like Maths and Chemistry, where I was above average, God only knows. I felt like I was chasing my parents' love and not getting it. That invisible wall seemed impenetrable and insurmountable, no matter how hard I tried or how well I did at home or in school with my band.

Once, when I was being whipped by my father, I cried out: "I love you dad! Why are you beating me?", which only led to a more ferocious lashing. On occasions, the shock and pain would cause me to wet my pants. Anything was an excuse for a beating. I would be thrashed for my shoelaces being undone, for having sleep in my eyes after washing my face, or for having my shirt hanging out of my trousers. Consequently, I was always walking on eggshells. Even though I was academically bright, my father decided to take me out of school, saying that he wasn't prepared to support me any longer.

While I was in the band, I was earning more than my parents' combined earnings.

Now here I was, being told to go out and nonsensically work for comparative peanuts. Both my mother and head teacher opposed my father's decision, to no avail; his mind was made up. I didn't get the chance to sit for the seven GCE O' levels and three GCE A' levels required for university entrance and was forced to abandon the course of study at Christmas, five months short of the exam dates. Shattered dreams and ambitions led to more pain, anger and frustration, excruciating feelings that I kept to myself. I believe this kind of existence laid the foundations for my road to drug and alcohol addiction. "Were these my real parents? Had I landed on the right planet?" These questions surfaced in my mind, time and time again. From wanting to attend university as a Law student, I ended up leaving home at my father's request, to become a criminal instead.

My father had a saying, "Two crabs can't live in the same hole!" After months of wondering what he actually meant by it, a family friend and ex-tenant explained that it meant my father no longer wanted me to reside at home. For me, it was a house and not a home. Home is somewhere you look forward to going to and where one is relaxed and at peace. All my efforts had been sabotaged, just as he'd tried to sabotage and ruin my mother's career but had failed.

I missed singing with the band, which, by now, had replaced me with someone who had a brand new 100 watts Marshall PA System. The fans were pleading with me to return, as they said my replacement could dance but couldn't sing. They couldn't understand why I'd left the band and I was too ashamed and hurt to explain. Now I understand why family secrets are unhealthy and need to be voiced, instead of being suffered in silence.

Mum, God bless her, got me my first job with a trademark and patents company, Abel and Imray on Chancery Lane, which ironically is where all of the Law Chambers are located. Talk about so near yet so far away. Here, I had the prospect of becoming a trademark and patent agent, with my own office and secretary, and was shown the other offices worldwide that would be open to me if I chose. I replaced the young man in the post room as post room clerk, with the responsibility for all files and post. In the afternoon, we all had cream cakes with our tea, at the company's expense. I got the job of distributing the cakes at teatime.

I was sacked from that job after spending six weeks away, playing around with my friends in the park during the summertime. I felt remorse, guilt and shame at letting my mother and myself down. The company ceased to send any wage packets to my home, where I'd been managing to intercept the post before my parents got wind of the situation.

Chapter 3

A Mother's Love

Mamie caught me in the act of leaving and said the only way she'd let me go was on the condition that I gave her my forwarding address. She understood my suffering and my determination to leave because of the "two crabs can't live in the same hole" declaration. I'd planned my exit and ordered a minicab for my journey to Knatchbull Road, in Camberwell Green, before anyone got home, but Mamie took me by surprise. Was it our ever-strong and loving bond that brought her to the house at the time of my departure? Yes! I think it had something to do with it.

Mamie was a spiritual woman and when I ventured into the unknown south of the river, feeling lost, rejected and all alone, she visited me once and brought me some pots and pans.

On another occasion, I met my mother as I got to the bottom of the escalator at Piccadilly Circus. She was about to ascend the station, on her way to work, and I'd been clubbing all night and was on my way home. I felt her sadness and acceptance of the situation as she told me: "Vander, if you can't be good, be careful!" She said it with the love I so dearly missed at home.

I felt she knew that I was up to no good. I always referred to her as Sherlock Holmes, since she had always been so good at detecting things that were going on with me. She often made me laugh, as I couldn't hide anything from her. Mama Jean loved me alright, but the situation at home made it difficult for everyone. My heart rose to my throat at my mother's wise and loving words and somehow, I managed to respond with the words: "I will." That's all I could manage as I continued on my way to the Northern Line while she ascended the escalator.

My path into crime was fuelled by anger, rage and resentment at my lost childhood and at the savage beatings I received for no reason. It was also compounded by the fact that I owed six weeks' rent and needed to eat and maintain myself. Pride prevented me from asking my mum or Mamie for help, although I had quit my electrical engineering job and wasn't receiving any state benefits at the time. Going to night school to finish my studies was out of the question, as I struggled to stay afloat, with all the mental and emotional baggage.

What began as one robbery, to resolve my domestic and personal difficulties, became a way of life, as I succumbed to the corruption of quick money, which didn't always come easy. My first partner in crime was a notorious hothead by the name of Titus, who saw me as the brainy one, from the school we had both attended. He relied on my leadership, which I found odd, since I saw him as the one with criminal experience. He'd already served time in approved schools and borstal and was hardly ever in school. I put him up after his parents threw him out and warned him that I'd do the same if he didn't do his fair share of the housework. I occupied a large room, kitchen diner and bathroom at the top of the house and he'd have to use the kitchen diner while I used the bedroom when we brought girls back to the house.

My work experience at home came in really useful in my new surroundings. My fear of rejection not only prevented me from asking for help, but also hindered me from asking certain girls for a date because my foolish pride would get deflated if the answer was no. I know now that "no" isn't a rejection, it's simply freedom of choice. But then, I thought it meant rejection and I thought rejection or the "no" word made me look weak.

The proceeds of my first crime paid off my rent arrears as well as the rent for a month or two in advance. I bought all the food I liked, which I didn't get at home on a regular basis. I bought new shoes and got made-to-measure tonic mohair suits. Furthermore, I bought a crate of Teacher's Whiskey and an ounce of ganja and dedicated my life to partying every day and night, to compensate for my lost childhood. A sign of my addictive trait? Yes! I certainly think so. Raving in shebeens, nightclubs and blues dances was a nightly affair until I was arrested for robbery, losing all my belongings as well as my liberty in the process.

The detective in charge of my case told the Bow Street Magistrate Court that although it was my first time in trouble as a teenager, he objected to bail because I had a wardrobe full of mohair suits and material possessions that were far too expensive for a sixteen-year-old.

I thought I'd go crazy in there as I struggled to accept and get used to my incarceration. I realised all the bragging and boasting about prison existence was a lie, as there was no enjoyment in prison. I was so delusional that when I was remanded into custody for the first time, I thought Ashford Remand Centre was a big house, with a wire fence around it. I was wrong, as the shock to the system hit home, with twenty-three hours lock-up every day, except for one hour of exercise, and an extra hour in the prison workshop, if you got picked.

After a month or two, I was put in a single cell and thought how the hell I was going to survive without company. In reality, I quickly got used to it as I got into a routine of reading and writing letters and cleaning up my cell. Night and day, we'd have competitions representing different sound systems, as we sang through the prison bars. Singing kept me sane, strong and optimistic about what lay ahead.

After seven and a half months, I was tried at The Old Bailey, in the notorious court number one. I was sent home to my father's house with a fifty pounds fine, on account of time spent in prison and being of previous good character. I was convicted based on the information given in Titus' statement. In disbelief, anger and disgust, we drifted apart as friends in HMP Ashford and even further apart when he was sentenced to Borstal Recall. I was too numbed and sickened to attack Titus over the matter.

My father and I didn't last long after he threw the mattress from his bed into the garden for burning, when he discovered

I'd had sex on it with my girlfriend. My mother wasn't living with him anymore and had filed for divorce while I was in prison. The girlfriend in question was called Peggy, and although we parted company soon after, she became the mother of my first son, JaJa, many years later.

I was compelled to leave my father's house with immediate effect and luckily found a room to rent that very day in an African's house in Clapton Pond. My tenancy was short-lived after the landlord questioned me about prison in a hallway that was constantly dark. In fact, the whole house seemed to be in darkness and felt spooky. As it transpired, they'd entered my room in my absence, found my prison letters and left the bone of an animal with raw flesh on it at the foot of my bed. I instantly vacated the building and found a place in Thistlewaite Road, with a nice Jamaican family. Being Jamaican herself, Peggy was given free access to my room in my absence via the landlord's keys. The security situation troubled me deeply and I had polite words with the landlord about it. He made light of everything, as he was a humorous and upbeat man and said he wouldn't do it again.

As I lay in bed with a blonde I'd met at a blues dance, DJ'd by Chicken Sound, I heard my window being pushed up by someone, as Peggy's leg protruded into my room at the front of the house. I rose instantly to meet the intruder in my birthday suit, with the blonde in a state of shock. I told Peggy she'd taken an unsanctioned liberty, as I recalled how she was unfaithful to me in prison and visited me only once in seven and a half months, and only when Mamie brought her at my request.

Peggy lunged at me with a fork and surprised me by stabbing me in my right leg. I overcame her all the same and threw her out. The blonde got dressed and left. I had two girlfriends and then, suddenly I had none. That incident reminded me of fights I'd had in prison that ended in isolation in the punishment block, sentenced to so many days on bread and water.

One of those fights was triggered by an inmate, incarcerated on the floor above our cell, who kept throwing shit parcels through the prison bars that landed on the ground outside my window, in the heat of summer. I was raging and wouldn't stop until I found the idiot responsible for the stink outside my window. In those days, we had to use the pisspot in our cell for such emergencies, so you can understand why I preferred a single cell. I steamed into the offender with both hands and feet, with Titus in tow, and felt no regrets about the punishment meted out by the prison governor. It was that incident that got me into a single cell after I was released from the block into the main wing. For the first time, I discovered how much I really enjoyed my own company.

From Thistlewaite Road, Clapton, London, Hackney, E5, I became a rolling stone, as I moved from one room to another. I felt like a tree without roots, like a leaf blowing in the wind. Although I was free from my father's aggression, I was a tortured soul, laughing and joking as if I was having a good time. Of course, I enjoyed myself to the best of my ability but the void and pain within was always there. It was a condition that began from the moment my parents left me to go to England and grew greater when I had to leave my beloved island of Dominica.

Another robbery charge saw me off to borstal after I stole the wages that were about to be distributed to factory workers on a Friday. My accomplice, Willy, turned informer after someone else told the police of our location. The moment I got bail, I gave that guy, Nat, a good hiding. As for Willy, I didn't touch him. He had bragged and boasted about his criminal abilities and connections, only to find himself reduced to tears as he knelt in my cell, at the notorious Hackney Police Station, spilling the beans to the police officers in our case. Needless to say, we became strangers after that, and I still don't know why I didn't give him a good hiding as well.

The police never recovered my share of the loot, which I hid in a strangers' garden shed, without their knowledge, during the police chase that followed the robbery. They visited me on a couple of occasions to find out where the money was hidden, but never recovered it. The only reason we got bail was because Willy's mum hired the services of a top QC (Queens Council) to defend his case. I remember that the Old Street Magistrate was like putty in the QC's hands.

At the Old Bailey, Willy was given two years' probation, as he managed to pass himself off as a teenaged first offender, when he was really over twenty-one years of age. Although I really was a teenager, I found myself sentenced to two years imprisonment. My barrister was hopeless and said nothing to mitigate my case when I changed my plea to guilty after Willy's statement. It was the clerk of the court who came to my defence, when he told the judge he couldn't sentence me to prison, as I wasn't yet twenty-one. He suggested I be sent to borstal instead. The judge was adamant that I go to prison but relented when he was told that it was a point of law on the statute book. Even the prosecution agreed, but my barrister said nothing.

From HMP Wormwood Scrubs I was sent to Morton Hall, supposedly a borstal for intelligent criminals. I excelled there in sports and broke the dead-lift weightlifting record that hadn't been broken in over ten years. I was simply enjoying myself in the gym when the physical trainer looked at me with eyes wide open and declared that I'd broken the record. I wanted to lift more but we'd run out of time and that borstal ran a strict regime, like the army. In fact, it was an air force base where the wings were named after pilots from the Dam Busters. I was in Learoyd Wing and there were Hannah and Gibson wings. We were located way out in the sticks in Lincolnshire, about three hundred miles from London. It was an open borstal and most guys who ran away were found roaming in the woods days later, as they went round in circles.

I bullied all the bully-boys in borstal and protected the bullied, although some of the bullies were bigger than me. I carried on singing and grew to appreciate the clean, fresh country air and fresh produce from the neighbouring farms we ate every day. I defended my friend Slue, who came from Birmingham. He worked in the kitchen and would bring me extra food to eat at nights on the wing. Slue later ended up as a chef for Steel Pulse, a talented Brummie reggae band.

I also befriended and defended a pint-sized, slim little fellah by the name of Bacon. He was a white boy from

Leicester, loved black music and liked to imitate the Jamaican accent. He was very fond of using those swear words that go with it. His cell and clothing were always untidy, no matter how hard he tried. I made sure that the racist white bully-boys stayed well clear of him.

I'd go on the football field during recreation and upset their game by grabbing the football and kicking it far away from the pitch. I'd get them to buy me sweets and tobacco from the canteen with their wages. Those whom I defended, only gave me things of their free will.

One racist officer who hated Bacon knew what was going on and vowed to get me back in some way. I smiled and simply said that all I was doing was defending the weak and vulnerable. He didn't like that. As borstal was a six months to two years' sentence, my intention was to get out as soon as possible. I did exactly that and learned to paint and decorate to the highest level, developing skills which included sign writing, wood graining, marbling and stencilling on walls. Mr Hirst was a great teacher and taught us the theory of painting and decorating at nights, while doing the practical stuff by day. Plumbing was my first choice, but there were no vacancies at the time. Mr Hirst said he was preparing us to decorate Buckingham palace and top-notch houses and mansions as well as to start our own painting and decorating business.

He was a jovial fellow and I enjoyed his tutorship. I received glowing reports at the end of every month from Mr Dawson, the officer assigned to my profile on the wing. We got on great, as I led our team to many victories in football, rugby, cricket and even table tennis, which was my weakest sporting link. I was surprised at how much I enjoyed rugby and was called the Wild Boar by the governor of Hannah wing. They encouraged me to go professional, and the same thing applied to boxing, where the trainer saw me skilfully handle his favourite boy boxer at the time, a heavyweight, while I was more of a middleweight. That heavyweight was also a bully, whom I had to chastise one day outside the dinner hall, to make sure that he left my friend Slue alone.

During my stay, our wing became the wing to beat in sport. Our wing governor, Mr Dunne, as he read through my files, said he couldn't understand how an intelligent young man like myself could end up in such a position. "If you want to be a successful criminal, you must associate with those who don't get caught!" he exclaimed. He encouraged me to mix with successful people in the profession of my choice in order to succeed myself. I never forgot his words.

On the wing, you'd mostly find me in the music room listening to Al Green, James Brown, Otis Redding (a favourite singer), The Wailers and many more great artists from the realm of black music. Most of all, I listened to 'Let's Stay Together' by Al Green as I yearned for the company of a woman and looked forward to dancing and romancing on my release. If not in the music room, you'd find me in the snooker room, which I dominated by scattering the balls of the bully-boys.

On one occasion, I head-butted a guy who thought he could walk over the freshly mopped floor, which was one of my assignments in my early days. After making an offensive remark, he ran off, with me in hot pursuit. I lost him, but eventually found him in the snooker room, where I took the cue from him before grabbing him and following through with a head-butt. As soon as I let him go, he fell to the floor and I took that as an opportunity to tell all inmates present that they'd all get the same if they messed with me.

I was grateful for books, letters, the Christmas parcel and visits from my mum and stepfather, Clive. They'd travelled over three hundred miles in the winter snow to see me, and that really pulled my heartstrings, as I didn't expect them to make that journey. Thank you, Mama Jean and Papa Clive!

I had sacked my girlfriend Peggy prior to my court case, telling her that I didn't want a repeat performance of her indifference. She had scarcely bothered writing or visiting, a sad state of affairs, compounded by her wilful infidelities. She certainly didn't plead or cry!

To my surprise, a beautiful sexy blonde by the name of Barbara, whom I considered the most elegantly dressed lady in the East End of London, wrote to me every day. We had kissed and even went to the cinema once, but never actually gotten around to further intimacy. Her father was an East End villain, who ensured that his little princess was the best dressed girl in town. Her daily letters gave me a welcome boost as I fantasised about her in the music room to 'Let's Stay Together'. She always attended the Chicken Blues Dance and was always one of the most dapper and beautiful ladies there. Thank you, Barbara!

The moment came when I was made head boy on the wing, and soon after, I was offered a chance to attend the Lincoln Show Jumping Events that I saw on TV. Bacon and I were teamed together, and I gladly accepted the opportunity, which involved re-erecting the fences that were knocked down. It began to rain on one particular day and the man who supervised us suggested we sit in his car until the rain cleared, while he trudged away somewhere. Bacon and I both sat in the back of the car. Suddenly, I saw Mr Robinson, the same officer who said he'd get me one day, wandering around as if looking for someone. I got out of the car immediately, calling and waving to indicate where we were. He ran towards us and declared that we'd attempted to escape. I looked at him in disbelief, wondering how someone could be so wicked without cause. He wasn't the least bit interested in finding the supervisor to corroborate our story.

On our return to borstal, we were immediately put down the block, where we awaited trial by our wing governor. Before that happened, little Bacon slashed his wrists and was immediately moved out of the cell next to mine and presumably taken to the hospital. The prison officers refused to enlighten me about anything. In fact, you weren't even allowed to talk down the block, and you stood all day until night-time, when your bed was put into the cell.

I explained to Mr Dunne that I hadn't yet learnt to drive (which was true) and that I wasn't even in the car when I called to Mr Robinson. Furthermore, we had no car keys and the engine wasn't even running, as Bacon sat in the backseat, out of the rain. I also argued that he get the supervisor's take on events before sentencing me and insisted that I'd been the victim of a cunning plot to sabotage my release date, which was in the following month and that the whole thing was a sick joke.

Mr Dunne smiled and even laughed as he read my statement, declaring he was impressed by what I said but he had to stand by his officer. As a result, my release date was cancelled, but I was released from the block immediately. Mr Dunne sounded almost apologetic and embarrassed by his officer's actions, which were clearly corrupt.

On the wing, I again enquired about Bacon and was met with a wall of silence, which made me fear the worst. I never saw that dear, scruffy little man again and remained haunted by the circumstances of his departure for some time. God Bless you Bacon.

On my return to borstal from home leave, I met a lovely girl on the train, with whom I exchanged addresses, but nothing came of it. I was the fittest I'd ever been, thanks to the fresh air, fresh food and sporting exercises. My release date was a month later than the original date and I left borstal, wearing a Prince of Wales check jacket and grey trousers, which I had chosen from the prison catalogue.

Chapter 4
Making Music or Doing Time

I noticed the air pollution as soon as I arrived at King's Cross and immediately yearned for the country air. I was hungry for advice, guidance and recognition from my elders. However, hanging around a squat, filled with a huge sound system called Sir Fray, replete with ganja dealing and all sorts of shady characters, didn't provide much guidance on clean, straight and sober living, but I enjoyed it to the max. Yet, deep within, I had to admit that I felt empty and alone. I was surrounded by pimps, whores, robbers, burglars, knifemen, axemen, gunmen, pickpockets, fraud artists, thieves, conmen, and killers. Among them were would-be musicians, singers, MCs, sportsmen and businessmen. Later, some of them even became world boxing champions, world-class footballers, pop, soul or reggae stars. I admired how certain individuals made the transition, but found it difficult to do the same, getting caught up in various criminal activities.

I met a wonderful lady called Suzanne, at Richmond Road Youth Club. She fitted my life like a glove and showed me unconditional love and loyalty. Her beautiful face was adorned with freckles, and she was from Irish stock. I made sure that she stayed well away from that squat but would take her to Sir Fray's blues dance, which was promoted by a brother called Clyde, and myself.

I stayed briefly at my father's house in Victoria Road, Leytonstone. During that short stay, I was paid a visit by a friend of mine called Luke, from Nottingham. He was on the run from Morton Hall, where we'd first met. Wearing a black trilby, long, black double-breasted Burberry raincoat, multicoloured platform shoes and a ring on every finger, he was hardly inconspicuous. His humour was constant and very entertaining.

Several evenings later, I was met with a solemn face as I entered the house, after a day's work as maintenance painter-decorator at Berkertex House on Oxford Street. Apparently, Luke had been arrested for looking suspicious as he gazed through the window of a jewellery store on Leytonstone High Road. My father refused to have him back at his house. Unwilling to let him go without an address, the police eventually discovered that he was on the run. My father was unrepentant about his decision, as he expressed his anger and disappointment at my choice of friends.

With empathy for Luke and embarrassment at my father's take on events, I went to see him at Wormwood Scrubs Prison, after taking the afternoon off work. More embarrassment followed some weeks later. My father demanded that I leave his house by sunset as I lay in my room with Suzanne, listening to Bob Andy's *Song Book* album, my favourite track being 'The More You Give to Life is the More You Gonna Get From Life So Don't Count the Cost'.

My father said his girlfriend, who had moved in with her son, was unwilling to launder my clothes or cook my food. I said I was happy to do these things for myself. However, he remained adamant about his decision. I never thought my father would put a woman and her son before his own.

I moved to Mamie's, at 30 Brighton Road in Stoke Newington N16 that very day and introduced Suzanne to her for the first time. Everyone saw how much Suzanne loved me and respected that. Even Blacks, who didn't believe in mixing with Whites, respected our relationship, for such is the power of unconditional love. I had to sleep in Mamie's room, on the couch, while Verina occupied the room next door. We were joined by my brother Glen, who needed a place to stay, and suddenly, we were as we were in Dominica, in less exotic surroundings. I moved out with Suzanne, who instantly left her mother's house, as soon as I found a room on Graham Road in Hackney E8.

The first thing I did was to install a huge Bang & Olufsen stereo sound system, which I'd bought from Tottenham Court Rd. Suzanne occasionally became my partner in crime, committing fraud, theft and con-artistry. God forgive me for that! And I trust that she has forgiven me as often as I've had to forgive myself for many things. Somehow, I kept writing songs, recording them a cappella, or over Studio One reggae instrumentals when I didn't have musicians to work with. I was offered a recording contract by PYE Records at Marble Arch, on the strength of my a cappella recording. I had bluffed my way into the A&R Department, claiming I had an appointment. After listening to my songs entitled 'Visions', 'Girl in This World' and 'L.O.V.E.', the man declared I was Britain's answer to Marvin Gaye. I agreed to come back and sign a contract after I got a musician to put some guitar riffs or piano sound behind the lyrics.

But I never returned. Putting financial and material gain before my music resulted in my arrest for robbing a bank and assaulting police. At the Old Bailey, the doctor's report from HMP Brixton revealed that I had suffered thirteen head injuries and many body blows. The robbery charge was reduced to theft in court and everyone, including the police, Suzanne and myself, thought I'd be freed as soon as the not-guilty verdict for assault on police was announced. However, that would've meant that they had assaulted me on a derelict site as I tried to make good my escape.

Two guilty verdicts resulted in a two-year, nine-month sentence. Although I had expected an acquittal, I was obliged to accept that this went with the territory. I was allocated to Maidstone Prison, where I reflected on the fact that my greed and impatience to buy an Aston Martin by dishonest means had sabotaged my opportunity in the music business. It was painful realising that I had to put music before shopping on Bond Street, buying fancy cars, night clubbing, bed-hopping or staying in five-star hotels for months at a time. I wanted it all at once, instant gratification, another addictive trait. Had I been found guilty of robbery, it could have resulted in a five-to ten-year sentence, depending on the judge's mood.

Suzanne stood by me, writing every day and visiting at every opportunity, whilst Mama Jean sent me esoteric and political books to read. Once again, my family was picking up the pieces, but with Suzanne on board, they had less to do.

I loved music so much that I couldn't understand why I didn't abjure criminality, as I could've had a comfortable lifestyle without putting my liberty on the line. I felt regret, anger, shame and frustration when I realised I could've acquired an Aston Martin honestly, making music instead of doing time. I told God I'd renounce violence and dishonesty if I were granted parole.

I was allocated a job in the wood workshop, where we built furniture. I attended gym regularly but never used the open-air swimming pool. I never saw an inmate use it whilst I was there. I felt that was because we had no confidence in the health and safety aspect of the water in the pool.

In my anger and despair, I pushed an inmate by the name of Barry. He knew I was behind him and was walking really slow on purpose. I was in no mood for this and acted as if I had somewhere really important to go. Suddenly, he caught me in the face with a punch. My boxing skills automatically kicked in and I subjected him to a flurry of punches, followed by some violent footwork. The prison officers got between us, but I still struggled to shake them off and finish the fight. Down the block, the governor was surprisingly lenient and let me back on the wing with a fine. I saw that governor many years later on TV. His transformation from a prison governor into a priest was the subject of a very interesting documentary about the prison service. I wasn't entirely surprised by his transformation after the leniency and compassion he'd shown me back in the day.

I was on Kent Wing where I became friends with an inmate by the name of David. He was built like a bear and was taken aback when I entered his cell to applaud him on the fine oil painting he was creating at the time. He was mixed race and assured me that no one walked into his cell unannounced, and he respected my courage for doing so. He accepted my compliments on the African beauty he was painting, and we became good friends.

It transpired that his current girlfriend, whom he loved madly was Barbara, a beauty from Whitechapel. He was concerned about her seeing another man in his absence and asked me if I knew the man in question, someone by the name of Martin. I said yes but I didn't divulge any information about him being part of the Chicken Sound Crew, nor anything about my brief liaison with her or the pen-pal relationship I had with her in borstal. I felt that I'd found something better in Suzanne. I didn't worry about her fidelity now that she had returned to her mother's place and secured a job.

Nonetheless, I found myself slipping into darkness again, until a small, white villain called Gary introduced me to yoga and meditation. Combined with weightlifting exercises and jogging, within two weeks I felt much lighter, as if I was walking on air. I really appreciated the benefits and thanked Gary for his tuition and support.

Maidstone was known as the drug prison, and it truly lived up to its name. I had no sooner arrived, when a white brother, by the name of Tony, entered my cell as I was unpacking my bed kit and left a generous piece of black hash on my locker by way of introduction.

The whole wing was awash with drugs, especially hashish. There was Moroccan, Afghani Black, Nepalese Temple Balls and Paki Black. There were also acid tablets, which I tried twice. I smoked hashish every day, due to the copious amounts available on the wing. I smuggled in money instead of ganja, which was my favourite smoke, as I didn't want Suzanne to get in trouble.

While I was smuggling money in on visits, dealers were smuggling money out, from the proceeds of the huge parcels that were dropped amongst the flowerbeds by certain visitors en-route to the visiting hall. These parcels were recovered by individuals in the gardening crew, who were paid for their services by those to whom the parcels belonged.

I did extra exercises with David on the wing in the evenings, in the bath and shower area, and this was always followed by spliffs and lemon tea. The smell of hashish was everywhere, even in the visiting room that turned into a cinema one night on the weekends. This was where David and I drank lemon tea with our spliffs. The prison officers paid no attention to the fragrance of hash, as long as we didn't smoke it in front of their faces.

I attended night school where I studied Accounting as well as Handbag Design and Manufacturing. Suzanne brought me a large roll of python snakeskin left at the bedsit. A few months later, I presented her with an exclusive handbag on visiting day. I attended a City & Guilds course in welding and also took up Economics and English at GCE 'A' Level. I intended to put right opportunities lost at school. Then, lo and behold, I was granted parole. The welding instructor said I'd gained enough knowledge and practice to start my own business as a welder or to apply for a job, although I wouldn't be able to take the exam. My tutors on the GCE courses arranged for me to sit my exams at a place on Oxford Street and I thanked them for that.

Chapter 5

An Angel from Dominica, and Mick Jagger

I bade many inmates farewell the night before my release. A smiling Suzanne was the first thing I saw as the prison door opened to introduce me to the outside world. We went to a hotel at my suggestion, instead of heading to Maidstone train station. We made love for hours before heading back to London the same day. Our lovemaking was fuelled with great passion and champagne, which I splashed all over her body.

Mama Jean let us an empty property she owned at Sudbury Hill. My sister Heather moved in a spare room sometime later with her boyfriend, Donovan. I continued with my yoga exercises but failed to turn up for my exams. Yet another example of my addictive traits sabotaging opportunities in my life.

One opportunity that I didn't sabotage was a job with a Trinidadian steel band, secured through Frank, my sister Verina's boyfriend at the time. Frank was a good man, and I'm sure he still is. I thought Verina was crazy to leave him and I'm sure that she's regretted it at some point.

I commenced rehearsals by playing the bass drums and eventually moved to other percussion instruments. We were billed to play as a supporting act to the Rolling Stones on their opening night at Earl's Court and in the foyer area for gigs afterwards.

We met Mick Jagger to discuss arrangements prior to our performances. The potent and pungent aroma of my spliff assailed everyone's nostrils; then, Mick suddenly looked at me and asked for a puff. I gladly handed him the joint, which he thankfully returned. Clearly, money, fame and adoration hadn't swelled his head. His feet were on the ground. I was humbled by the fact that he took time out to discuss certain details with us personally. I learned a lot from his example. Thank you, Mick!

On the night that we performed on stage to a full house, I was still standing there with maracas in hand, after everyone else had left the stage. I loved it up there! The stage manager quietly ushered me backstage. The Stones were brilliant, night after night, with the magic of Ollie Brown on percussion, and Billy Preston on keyboards.

I began reading the Bible and when I got to Numbers, Chapter Six, I decided to dedicate my life to God. Eventually, we moved to Wandsworth, where I continued to study the Bible every day. I told Suzanne I was done with the dishonesty and violence and wasn't clear about what I'd do for a living, as I focused on the divine word. She asked me to let her join me on my spiritual journey and to teach her what I understood. I declined her request and explained that I was only just learning myself. She could see that the changes in me were real and was baffled by my transformation, as we continued our relationship. My love for her was no less intense when I decided to put God first, stopped getting haircuts and shaving and changed my diet to fish and vegetables. The fish had to have scales and all crustaceans were out.

With a heavy heart, I asked Suzanne to leave me and to find herself a rich man. She asked me to reconsider my decision, but I remained adamant. Enraged by my decision, she smashed an antique I'd acquired and refused to return the diamond ring I gave her; although she found a rich man quickly enough. I told her that I needed the money from the sale of the ring to assist me through the lean times I was experiencing. She refused to return it, even though she was engaged to be married in a matter of weeks.

Again, she returned to ask me to reconsider my decision, before she took the plunge into marriage, but I stood firm. After making love to her in the flat I had moved into upstairs, we parted company outside Holborn Tube Station. She walked away angrily, as I stood there with a broken heart. I had broken hers and mine. How could I do such a thing to her and to myself after she stood by me in so many ways for so long? I had to put God first, came the answer. I walked in the rain for hours after that, with no sense of direction. Shortly after, I moved to Chelsea and then to Fulham by the river, and from there to Battersea.

After only days in Battersea, my flat was burgled, resulting in the loss of all my possessions. These included my favourite Bang & Olufsen Hi-Fi, all my clothes, my big record collection, all my socks, shoes and underwear and even my kitchen cutlery. I stood there in shock as I scanned my empty flat, realising that this was an act of hatred instead of an opportunistic theft. What hurt me most of all was the loss of a combination briefcase containing all my songs. I always boasted that it was my treasure chest filled with priceless jewels.

With my back against the wall, I slid down to the floor and smoked a spliff from the bud of marijuana that lay on my opened Bible. These were the only two things that were left behind. I took that as a sign. I'd never been burgled before. I felt my life had been violated and refused to live in that place. Disbelief and dismay turned to anger as I set out to avenge what had happened. I sought the help of Michael (MC), who'd also been released from Maidstone Prison, to help me find the culprits. It was his area and he knew who it was. I developed a deep loathing for burglars.

I trawled the streets armed with a large knife, fuelled by anger and hatred. I was determined to torture that guy, whom I had gotten to know as Tim, to compensate for the agony of the losses that had been inflicted upon me. I knew he was guilty because he had abandoned the home he shared with his baby-mother. I waited outside a cinema and other venues, lurking in the shadows like a predator, ready to pounce on the prey. I became frustrated, as the prey never materialised according to information received. Then one day, MC shouted, "There he is!" I got out of the car with knife in hand and headed towards him with tunnel vision, careful not to betray my purpose. Amid the suspense and excitement of closing in on my prey unawares, I heard MC cry out "Police". Disappointed and deflated, I returned to the car, after I heard him shout it for the second time.

Having searched for Tim for some two months, and not having any income, financial pressures began to take their toll. I knew I needed to get back to work. Then, later, I abandoned my search, after listening to a ballet dancing couple who became good friends of mine. Later, they moved to Scotland to live in a castle, where they continued teaching their discipline. After pouring out my soul to them with complete honesty, they helped me see my situation not as a setback, but as a life cleansing process, which offered me an opportunity to start afresh. They also left me an open invitation to visit them at the castle that came with their new job.

I decided to go into business selling ganja, the sacred herb. I remembered the bud that had lain in the centre of my Bible. I had dabbled with it before and took it as a reliable source of income. It felt good not to be robbing and stealing or getting violent with people, just to make a living.

I moved back across the river to Navarino Road in Dalston, Hackney, where I joined the Rastafarians and quickly became a name in the ganja business as I rose up the ranks.

I started a small record label entitled 'Jah Child', producing artistes such as Sugar Minnot, Trevor Hartly and The Heptones. I also embarked on producing less well-known artists such as Winston Fergus and worked with musicians such as Rico Rodriguez, erstwhile trombonist with the Skatellites; Angus (Drummie) from Aswad; Hughie Issachar; Alan Weekes, a lead guitarist-; and others from the reggae business at the time. I can assure all those other artistes, whose names I haven't mentioned, that they are regarded with the utmost respect. I was on a high, writing, singing and recording my own songs. I became a Rastafarian and as my locks grew, I embraced a strictly Ital (vegan) diet, smoked copious amounts of ganja in a water chalice, and reasoned with my brethren about God (Jah), the bible, life and black history. Reciting Psalms was an integral part of that experience.

I brewed ganja tea on a daily basis and included it in my vegan stews, home-baked cakes, steam puddings and porridge. I enjoyed these moments, with music playing on the reel to reel (the best sound in the world), as various women came in and went out of my life.

My stepfather, Clive Anderson, a music enthusiast, was a critic for magazines including 'Black Music & Jazz Review' and 'Let it Rock', with occasional contributions to the 'Caribbean Weekly Post'. He's also a compiler of Soul LPs and CDs, a master and teacher of the English language. He arranged an appointment for me with Red Bus Records on Oxford Street. I really appreciated his help and was looking forward to that appointment when I received a call from my solicitor, telling me that I was to appear at Chelmsford Crown Court on that same afternoon. I was gutted at missing the appointment. Something stank as he said I had to be there in less than two hours and offered to pick me up with his barrister father, to ensure that I got there on time. He then said that there was no way that they could cancel the case. Sadly, I remembered the last opportunity that I had sabotaged with PYE Records.

And so, at short notice, I was transported to the Crown Court, where I received eighteen months' imprisonment for possession of ganja that weighed much less than a quarter of a gram. I'd told my girlfriend, Cheryl, that I'd be back soon and intended to rebook another appointment with Red Bus Records at the earliest opportunity, but my fate had been sealed.

I'd changed my not guilty plea to guilty on my barrister's advice although the ganja wasn't found on my person, in my home or my car, but ten yards away from where I stood on the pavement. Down in the cells, I flung my gold chain at the barrister, along with a wad of cash as he spoke about appealing against the sentence. I recalled looking at him and his son in the front seat of the car as we rode to court. They looked like undertakers; in that attire they could easily pass as that. I had felt like stopping the car and walking away due to my sudden premonition but talked myself out of it by concluding that the worst that could happen was a fine.

I told him to give the chain and all the money he picked up from the floor to Rhoda, the mother of Immanuel and our twin daughters, Naomi and Makeda. She was pregnant with Nathaniel at the time.

Prior to my journey to court and not taking anything for granted, I'd swiftly made arrangements with my brother, Glen, to make weekly payments to Peggy and Rhoda.

The governor at Wandsworth Prison, which was feared more than any other prison in London, looked at me in shock at the severity of my sentence and asked me if I was appealing. "Yes, I am!" I replied. Finally, I paid a reputable firm by the name of Offenbach & Co to launch an appeal, after the father and son dragged their feet on the matter, causing me to appeal out of time, with good reason.

Being a vegan in Wandsworth Prison wasn't easy, although cannabis resin, marijuana and cocaine were readily available to me whilst I was there. I had to produce proof of my membership of the Vegan Society, while my girlfriend made calls to the Home Office to ensure that I was given my rights regarding my diet as well as get exempted from haircuts. HMP Wandsworth was notorious for cutting off a Rastaman's locks on his arrival at reception. The prison doctor checked me for malnutrition whilst I survived on potatoes, cabbage and water. Three months later, raw soya mince was added to my diet.

I became friends with a man serving a seven-year sentence for smuggling tons of hashish via his haulage company and respected how he supplied every wing with the said stuff. He had tea with the chief P.O. in the office overlooking the circle that separated the wings, upon which no prisoner was allowed to walk. Anyone who did so would be rained upon by a hoard of officers and carted to the block.

Don had the freedom to go from wing to wing and was out of his cell even when everyone else was locked up. Wandsworth was known as the no-nonsense prison, with regular twenty-four-hour bang ups. Disobedience to button up or tuck in your shirt resulted in a fast and furious trip to the block. I was upset at how long it took to wrestle my case from the old firm. Their reluctance to give up the case had ensured that I spent much longer behind bars than was necessary, as I was confident of winning my appeal.

As I walked around the exercise yard, I heard a voice say, "Hey V!" It was MC, his eyes peering through the bars of the prison block in the basement. Conversation wasn't allowed. However, our short verbal exchanges revealed that he'd just begun a fourteen-year sentence. He masked the burden of the years ahead with a defiant grin, as we wished each other well.

In a flash, I recalled a packed night in the Four Aces when a brother came in to declare that there was a man outside who wanted to see me. To my surprise, there was MC, sitting on the bonnet of a Spearmint Green Jaguar XJ6, looking upbeat like he'd just come into a lot of money. He said he had to let me know that the man who had emptied out my flat had been jailed for seven years as a result of another burglary. Then there was the time when he was a wanted man after escaping from a prison van on the way to court. My eighteen months paled into insignificance, but the sense of injustice remained.

I re-joined Lance around the yard after my brief encounter with MC. That's when he told me about the barrister and his solicitor son. It came as no surprise when Lance revealed to me that my original solicitor and his barrister father were working with the police to ensure that certain individuals were put behind bars and in return, they would be allocated a certain number of cases from the police station. I didn't question him. He was related to them and certainly didn't employ their services. I was just grateful for being informed about the situation. Offenbach came highly recommended and I trusted in their reputation, as I looked forward to my imminent release.

Lance and I were good friends. He was a small, articulate and elegantly dressed man who liked to drive Porsche and Mercedes cars. I enjoyed reasoning with him on spirituality, philosophy, history, politics, religion, current affairs and ways of making money. We prospered in our dealings although we once lost a six-figure sum by mistake. We also embraced every opportunity to play chess together during our confinement.

I had a hacker radio sent in by Peggy for my use. It was highly respected by other inmates for its heavy bassline and quality sound. I could have rented it out for tobacco or other goodies, including cannabis. There was no need for that. I used a hash pipe that I made from aluminium, smoked hashish and ganja, had the occasional line of coke and wrote many songs including 'Babel' and 'Concrete City'.

I was transferred to Spring Hill Prison on the Isle of Sheppey, with its solitary bridge linking it to the mainland. The prison had an open and closed section. I was allocated to 98 Block, the closed section, on a hill overlooking the open section, where prison visits took place.

After reading my report, the governor directed that I work in the kitchen, which wasn't easy to get into. At last, my diet was being treated with respect, as the officer in charge ordered vegan cheese, soya milk and soya mince on my behalf, while giving me the job of preparing and cooking the vegetarian diet. I was under no illusions that this was due to Mr Bowyer, the officer in charge of the kitchen, who appeared to be miserable most of the time, with his humpty dumpty physique, and not the governor. Mr Bowyer watched us like a hawk, in a bid to prevent us smuggling out sugar and cuts of meat etc. to other inmates, for which we could charge a fee. I didn't get involved in that sort of thing, although others did.

Hyped up as the vegetarian prison chef, I ordered seasoning that they didn't have such as curry, paprika, and whole-wheat flour for the pastries. I prepared and cooked vegetable chow mein, seasoned rice and vegetables, and stuffed peppers. The kitchen and dining area was suddenly filled with the aroma of home cooking. Nearly half of the inmates turned vegetarian. The boss didn't like it and said, "Vander, this is a prison kitchen, not a restaurant!" and urged me to cut out the fancy stuff. I carried on the same way as usual and was demoted to only being allowed to prepare vegetables and cook my own food. The other inmates were gutted.

Another inmate, Ron, who had his own coach business, was finding it hard to come to terms with his sentence for acting as a getaway driver, claiming that he was innocent and had unknowingly given two robbers a lift. He sold cannabis resin on my behalf. I didn't want any money, only things like peanut butter, drinking chocolate and other goodies from the canteen. I shared the proceeds with him, which ensured that my cupboard was constantly well stocked. I smoked hash in the morning before work, in the afternoons on break and every night.

Offenbach and Co. proved very efficient and before I knew it, I was summoned to the Royal Courts of Justice on appeal. Just prior to that, while I was still working in the kitchen, the gaffer called me to his office and declared, "You've got a boy!" as he came off the phone in earshot of other inmates. We all celebrated with a drink of cocoa.

Cheryl came with Rhoda and baby Nathaniel to see me, on my request, and produced a golden silk and satin embroidered, hand-stitched dressing gown that she had tailored for me, in order to get my response. I wondered if Nathaniel was really my son, as I'd only slept with Rhoda once before she became pregnant. Despite the dark clouds of doubt that overshadowed the proceedings, I was delighted to see them. I admired Cheryl's handiwork and expressed my enthusiasm to wear the gown as soon as I returned to freedom.

Rhoda was a tall, beautiful, slender lady, African-English mixed race, a little shy and softly spoken. I wished that I could have gone home to her and the four children, but I was in love with Cheryl. As a matter of fact, Rhoda rejected me when I revealed I wasn't in love with her in the same way as I was when we first met.

Cheryl was of Asian-Caribbean descent, slender, lovely and outgoing. I was to set her up with a solicitor's office in St Lucia as soon as she passed her Law degree. I had also financed a six weeks holiday for her in Grenada with her girlfriends, while I was waiting for my appeal. I asked her to wait for me since I would soon be out on appeal, but she was determined to go with her friends, and I did not stand in her way.

Needless to say, I won my appeal without a word being said by my beautiful barrister, Miss Scotland. I was surprised to see that she was black, I had imagined her to be white before our meeting. When she rose to speak to the three judges, she was told that her representation was not necessary as they'd already made up their mind and I was to be released the following day. "Why not release me now?" I thought. What was the point of going all the way back to prison on the coast when I was already in London, where I lived? All the same, it was a relief to hear the judges' words. I thanked the young and beautiful Miss Scotland, who said, "Vander, don't thank me, thank yourself. Your written statement to the judges caused them to reach an early decision."

Years later, during my disastrous marriage to Michelle, I saw that beautiful lady on television, being introduced as Baroness Scotland, originally from Dominica. I regretted not asking her out long ago, at our meeting, when she disclosed to me that we were from the same island. The only title I could have given her then would have been Mrs and not Baroness. I wondered what would have happened had we gotten together. She was a really decent lady and deserves her title.

Chapter 6

From Brotherly Love
to Crackhead Hell

My brother, Glen, came to pick me up in a white BMW and gave me an ounce of sensimilla to celebrate the appeal win. I rode home on a cloud in the backseat, like a bird freed from the cage.

I thanked my brother for making sure the money I had left in his care had gone towards supporting my children in my absence. He was, and still is, a tall handsome man, with looks like a mega star from Hollywood. "My pleasure!" he exclaimed. A tough but gentle soul, he was a real ladies' man, who put his family first, and worked hard for a living in a large Hi-Fi store in Tottenham Court Road. Later, he became manager of a quality Hi-Fi store in Whitechapel. He had the gift of the gab and was a great asset to any company he worked with, including Heals Furniture Store in Sloane Square, Chelsea. His home was furnished with their classic productions, which included lighting and other fittings. He was clean, sober and honest. Loved and liked by everyone, he had married at the age of seventeen, after producing a wonderful son, Curtis, with Nina, the daughter of the famous Maestro Pedro.

Pedro addressed everyone as "My Lord! My Lady! Duke and Countess". He raised peoples' self-esteem and self-worth everywhere he went with his impeccable manners. He had a unique style of dancing close up with the ladies at clubs 007, Four Aces, the Roaring Twenties in Carnaby Street and at Count Shelly; blues dances, which everyone attended like dukes and duchesses, elegantly attired for the occasion. He was the only man I saw who was never refused a dance by a lady even if she was with another man. Jovial, upbeat and a shining example, he moved amongst the gunmen, knifemen, robbers, thieves, conmen, pickpockets, pimps, prostitutes, ganja sellers and honest hardworking people who followed Count Shelly Sound. The Count himself was a huge man, highly respected, and a great asset to reggae and the music business with his Count Shelly label.

That reminds me of the times I used to sneak out my house, at the age of fourteen, through the bathroom window onto the kitchen roof, then along the garden wall, keeping my balance until I was perched above Well Street Common. There, I would pause and leap, making a soft and silent landing on the grass, before heading to Club 007, where I'd meet up with my best friend and blood brother, Hilton, who was in my class at school. Hilton didn't have to sneak out. He was an only child in a one parent family, with a lovely loving mother who bought him anything he asked for, including the made-to-measure green tonic mohair suit he wore. His suit was tailored at Roseman's in Dalston, around the corner from Club 007, whilst my light brown equivalent was tailored at David London on Mare Street, Hackney. I had to pay for it a little at a time, until I got it out of the shop. All the tailors were Jewish and were highly skilled at making suits to meet our individual requirements.

While I was writing these reminiscences, I discovered through Clive, my stepfather, that Mama Jean occasionally visited the Four Aces and so did he, although they never met there. Sometimes, the world is a small and perilous place and with unknown acts like Motown's Supremes putting in an early appearance, I could have been caught in flagrante delicto as I enjoyed these nocturnal adventures.

At Club 007, we'd rave the nights away to the exclusive sounds of Count Shelly and Sir Fray. Both DJs were good friends and it was Sir Fray who gave Count Shelly his break at the club. I admired and copied dance moves from the hustlers and gangsters who filled the floor. Club 007 was a huge crumbling building that must have been a credit to the architect in its day, with a grand staircase leading up to the main hall, where we danced till dawn, completely oblivious to the fact that one day Pedro would become my brother's father-in-law. The ganja smelt sweet although I hadn't started smoking anything at all at the time, not even cigarettes.

The 007 era came to an abrupt end when it was raided by the army and police because of its notoriety. I wasn't there when it happened. I always had to return home by the same method whilst everyone was still in bed. I thought it was my secret until, later on, my mother disclosed that she and my father had their suspicions of my clandestine operations on a Saturday night.

As I recall, Pedro was a gambler and womaniser who had won a substantial amount on the pools and lost it in gambling dens. The rest of the loot was reputed to be stolen after he was followed to the spot where he had hidden his winnings.

Glen returned the rest of the money I had left in his care. I told him I didn't mind if he'd helped himself to any of it. He said he didn't, and I believed him. I loved my brother deeply and wished that all my sisters were boys. It wouldn't have made any difference if he said he'd spent or invested it all anyway.

Pedro and his sons Bobby (no longer with us), Paul, and Michael and myself, were saddened by the breakdown of Glen's marriage to Nina. They all blamed Nina for the separation.

Around this time, I was introduced to cocaine at Wally's house. He was a gentleman, dangerous and flamboyant as well as a close friend. I said I'd never use cocaine and there I was, snorting lines of the stuff with him and his new acquaintance, Tony, who glorified the white stuff whilst making negative comments about sensimilla. That incident occurred sometime before my eighteen months' sentence.

This led me to smoke crack later on, a habit that was called freebasing at the time. I was unaware of the slippery and slimy slope on which I had chosen to live, oblivious to the destruction of self and others that lay ahead. The coke habit began as money flowed into my life in abundance. How it destroyed lives was unknown to me at the time because I thought addicts were only those people who injected drugs.

I tried to help one such individual I'd met in the kitchen of block 98, which was the closed section of HMP Spring Hill. His name was Dipstick, a pickpocket no doubt, but a sweet little fellow all the same. He had a similar energy to Bacon and reminded me of that dear friend whom I never saw again. I introduced him to sensimilla, hoping that it would help him leave heroin behind. Such was my naivety at the time. The word heroin conjured images of death, but I clung to the delusion that coke was different.

How could any substance that kept me awake for days, enabling me to drink gallons of booze without eating any food, be supporting my life? That habit was killing me softly and silently while I lived in denial of the fact. After all, it didn't declare that it was causing a disconnection from God, man, woman, and myself, as it led towards financial ruin and moral decay. At first, one gram lasted a week, then a weekend, and finally it developed into a daily habit. Soon after that, my interest in snorting coke decreased, as crack smoking became not just a habit, but an obsession and a compulsion that was practiced every night, till dawn. Suddenly, it also became part of my day and as a result, the curtains no longer allowed the sunshine in. My descent into addiction had truly begun.

Dipstick lived in a large squat in a mansion block in Kentish Town. I entered the gloom to find myself walking into an eerie silence, over bodies strewn on the floor. The bathroom and toilet walls were splattered with blood. I felt as if I was in a tomb instead of a flat and told him he'd have to meet me in Camden Town, at a flat in Chalk Farm in future. I was encouraged when he declared that he and his friends liked the sensimilla but became downcast when I noticed the pinprick pupils in his eyes. He ended up in the Whittington Hospital with pneumonia, as we gradually lost contact with each other.

Chapter 7

In Paradise – but Still Lost

On my release, I waited for my current girlfriend, Cheryl, to return from holiday in Grenada with her friends. Her friends returned but she didn't. Instead, I received long distance collect calls from her asking me to send her more money. I declined her request since I believed she'd found a gigolo and assured her that I'd be there within a week. I was true to my word.

My planned stop-over in Barbados was curtailed when I awoke to find that someone had entered my room and stolen about three thousand US dollars in cash from my wallet.

I was angry with that, but even angrier with my girlfriend. I landed in Grenada and immediately threatened her lover, which resulted in a meeting with his gang boss, in a house on Mount Parnassus. The fact that I had travelled thousands of miles across the ocean to get my girl made an impression regarding my seriousness of intent. The meeting was cordial and ended peacefully as they appeared to be on my side, even though I was a stranger. I believed God was protecting me.

I found her living in poverty with a lady in Cherry Hill. Thanking the woman for her kindness, I shared a humble meal with her and gave her gifts and money. Cheryl reluctantly moved in with me in a beach chalet on Grand Anse Beach, at the Silver Sands Hotel.

I was offered cocaine but declined, opting for ganja instead, and went through one-pound weight of the herb in about a fortnight. I wondered if I'd done the right thing or whether I should have left her to her folly. She'd been thrown out of the gigolo's mother's house when she ran out of money.

Apparently, she was looking for a teaching job whilst she was being housed and fed by a woman who earned about ten pounds a week.

From Grenada we flew to St Lucia. On the plane, I opened the large envelope I had left in the hotel safe to discover two thousand US dollars missing. Furthermore, the Bank of Nova Scotia refused to allow me to withdraw the money I'd banked with them and I had to wait many weeks before it was transferred to the Nova Scotia Bank in Castries, St Lucia.

After a spell at East Winds Hotel, I rented an apartment in Summersdale, just outside the capital, Castries. However, this proved short-lived because the landlord didn't like the characters that visited me since the day I moved in, and the smell of ganja smoking didn't help. As a result, I rented a mansion in Bonne Terre, overlooking Rodney Bay, where I assumed smuggling activities took place. I became part of the community and held a big party, where I befriended a pilot, local gangsters, artists, retired people and local businessmen. I even became a fixture at cultural activities in the town and country.

I prayed day and night, reasoning about God at every opportunity with like-minded people. What began as a four week stay, turned into a seven-month adventure, as I enjoyed the beauty of the island and its people. During that time, I visited Dominica twice: firstly, with my girlfriend and then, by myself whilst still maintaining my holiday home in St Lucia. I also managed to see some of Antigua, Martinique and St Vincent.

Visiting my father in Dominica was a healing process for me. I never asked him why he beat me as a child. I felt sure that he loved me from the way he showed concern for my safety, for there was considerable hostility towards Rastafarians on the island, politically as well as socially. That hurt me deeply, especially as the hatred was directed towards their own sons and daughters.

I sat on the mountain amongst the clouds with my cousin Lennox, who gave me graphic details of violence inflicted upon Rastas who lived in those mountains in peace, love and independence, a choice for which they were hounded, maimed and murdered.

Lennox himself had to cut off his locks when he became the most wanted man on the island on account of his ganja running activities. He cultivated and sold it by the ton. After cutting his hair, he became invisible and drove and walked past the police unrecognised. He lamented that there was no money in selling bananas as he dug up a tin of ganja, which we smoked while eating the sweetest and juiciest melon I've ever tasted. He grew bananas, fruits and vegetables on the same plot that had previously been covered by marijuana trees. This was the same mountain I'd aspired to climb as a child.

Leaving Dominica was a painful experience, but before I left, I witnessed the end of a rainbow very close to my father's house. I cherished the moments I spent at Picard River with my other cousin Aaron and spoke with my father about my intentions to buy some land by that beautiful river where we bathed.

On another occasion, I spent time by a river in Tatan, where I met some rastas. We picked mangoes by the riverside and washed them in the cool, fresh and clear waters. We bathed there under the radiant sunshine pouring from blue skies high above. I was introduced to an armchair that was naturally formed from a rock in the river, directly under the waterfall. We took turns relaxing there while the waters massaged every part of our bodies. It was an exhilarating experience. This was the same river Mamie and I had bathed in, at the point where it met the sea. I still remember Lennox's parting words when he said, "Vander, there's no money in bananas." The price of a box full of bananas meant that they had to fill thousands of boxes to barely survive! I had thought the days of slavery were over!

After leaving Dominica, I returned to St Lucia. Cheryl, who had accompanied me on the previous trip two months before, had refused to remove her head wrap at customs and was denied entry. My father got the Minister of Home Affairs to override their decision, but they became defiant and refused to obey the Minister's orders. It was just as well since she harboured two ounces of sensimilla in her head wrap.

Cheryl and I had a great time with a couple of American intellectuals, both Rastafarians, who had flown from Jamaica with their son and with another child on the way. They said they left because of the constant gunfire and found St Lucia much more peaceful. Later on, I discovered that they had defrauded a lot of people by computer hacking and travelled the world by the same method. They kept a large stash of thousand-dollar US bills in a bag meant for golf clubs and lived unassumingly in a poor area.

I invited them to shower over at my place, which they gratefully accepted, although I knew that they could easily afford to buy the mansion I lived in. We had a wonderful time touring St Lucia and I fondly remember trips to Soufriere, Sulphur Springs, Fonzu Jacque, Grosilet, Babooneh and many more places. Looking at Marigot Bay was like beholding heaven on earth, and to see the Rastafarians who lived among the bubbling lakes at Sulphur Springs was a mystical experience.

Chapter 8
Gunfire and Obsessing

On my return to England, I felt the darkness closing around me as the plane descended into Heathrow Airport and all the troubles I'd left behind came flooding back. It was insufferable, and I just had to get away. Within a week, I flew to Jamaica with Cheryl and my second son, Immanuel, in tow. I also bought a ticket for my first son, JaJa, who was travelling to Jamaica with his mother Peggy, and I planned to meet up with him in Lucy, in the parish of Westmorland. It was all about relaxing and enjoying the food and weather, with an eye and an ear open for business opportunities. The smell of crack cocaine crept out of certain hotel rooms and balconies, but I kept away from it all.

Again, that descent into Heathrow Airport had me thinking about the crack pipe and obsessing about that first hit that would transport me away from all my troubles and pain. Of course, that never happened, no matter how much I smoked and how long I kept at it. I would leave the crack pipe, exhausted after three days and nights without rest, and repeatedly swore I'd never do it again.

Yet the moment I woke up, I'd hear that glass pipe calling me from the cupboard under the kitchen sink. I thought, "I'll smash it next time!" Another voice would say, "Smoke it now and be done with it." Having coke around and the pipe waiting, I usually took the easier option, overwhelmed by the obsession and compulsion to use. Gripped by denial I'd say, "This will be the last time."

Cheryl would go out in the morning and return in the evening from college and would find me still at it, rooted to the same spot up to five days later. She said nothing, and I said nothing.

I'd sometimes be in the company of a brother nicknamed 'Slow Burner' by Wally, for his very laidback style of crack smoking. Wally was a friend with whom I used to make excursions to Wales and as far away as Jamaica. Slow Burner, otherwise known as Alan, was well connected with the robbery scene and would visit me as soon as he got his wages. Wally would pop in to see me when he ran out of coke and I would do the same, at sociable or unsociable hours.

We spent many sessions together, all dressed up as if we were going out on the town, only to end up sitting around a circular antique table at a Hampstead address, with hustlers and high-profile artists from the reggae business passing through. My friend would put down the torch and pipe on the table after exhaling a thick cloud that hung like a veil around our faces. The sound *shoosh* would invariably follow as the hit transported my friend, me or any of our colleagues around the table, into the twilight zone. The hit was known as the Humdinger at the time. Yes! That was where my crack smoking days began and there's no one to blame. I am responsible! The illusion was that we all thought we were having a good time, unaware of the dangers and consequences that lay ahead.

Well! When I met an American ex-racing driver, by the name of Ken, who was refurbishing a flat in Mayfair, I was wondering aloud about such consequences, he said that he had been freebasing since the sixties and knew people who had been doing it from even earlier. The fact that he appeared to be managing well at nigh on seventy, gave me the green light to stay in denial. It never occurred to me to ask him if crack had killed his racing career, which had ended prematurely.

I co-owned an Ital restaurant in London with Wally, and had further investments in a nightclub, another restaurant and a photography business outside London. Further investments in the pool table and electronic games business, combined with my record label, commanded respect from others that I didn't fully appreciate at the time.

As I approached my restaurant one day, I saw reggae artist Errol Dunkley, who had a big hit with 'Ok Fred' on the Count Shelly label. He stood on the pavement outside the premises, looking lost and trembling with fear. I hailed him to no avail. He looked at me, bemused, and walked away before I got close.

As soon as I entered the restaurant, the staff informed me that Errol had been shot at outside, by two men in a car. I was no wiser as to who the assailants were when I was questioned by the police soon after. I insisted that they question me in front of the customers and made it clear that I was unable to assist them with their enquiries, as I was not at the scene of the crime at the time. They implied that my arrival so soon after the event had cast a shadow of suspicion over me. They also indicated that the restaurant would be subject to regular visits, since I was being uncooperative. I responded by saying that they were welcome at the restaurant at any time, with food and drinks on the house. They left, and never returned for further questioning.

However, they tailed me from the restaurant one day, on my way to get some supplies from Baldwins, at Elephant and Castle. As a vegan restaurant, we cooked fresh menus every day. I'd hired Spirit and his van for the trip. As we rode past Liverpool Street Police station, we were halted at a set of traffic lights by a couple of Bobbies on the beat. Spirit instantly chewed and swallowed the huge burning spliff that was held between his lips at the time. I got out of the vehicle and threw some ounces of high quality ganja in front of the moving traffic. I then proceeded to chew the ounce of Black Hash I'd bought to send to Sir Fray, who was serving four years' imprisonment for intent to supply herbal cannabis.

Spirit and I were locked up for ten days in Mansion House Police Station, prior to being charged. He was charged for criminal damage, after he tore off a piece of sponge from the pillow in the cell in order to wipe off some water pooled on the bench. I was charged for possession of some Hashish and weed that they'd swept up from the road. As a result, we were both fined when we went to court. I knew that it was illegal to incarcerate us for so long without charging us, but I didn't pursue the matter. It later transpired that the men who shot at Errol Dunkley were two people I knew as Keith and Steve, who subsequently received jail terms.

After leaving my first session ever with the crack pipe, in Hampstead, I remember going home wishing I had taken some coke and a crack pipe with me. Then I struggled to get to sleep, for all I saw when I closed my eyes was the pyramid shaped bowl of the glass water pipe, full of a creamy white cloud of smoke that beckoned me to what I quickly began to identify as the twilight zone. Why would a sane person want to visit a spooky place like that, time and time again? I couldn't wait for the next session the following night.

In the twilight zone, car headrests became people's faces. The Bunsen burner had to be adjusted to burn silently low, or switched off, so that one could hear a pin drop. Peeping through the curtains became a habit, as paranoia took effect. Walking on tiptoes at three to five am in the morning, for fear of the neighbours hearing one's footsteps, became part of the ritual. I listened to the line to hear if the phone was bugged. Lusting after other women became obsessive, as I came to believe that coke and crack plus money could get me any woman I wanted. Then there was the action of abruptly getting up and rushing out of the house, in fear of Customs and Excise, and police surveillance, only to find out that it wasn't true.

I was in Easy Street Studios once, when I received a phone call from Cheryl, informing me that the second flat I had rented had been burgled. I didn't race to the scene but finished the recording session instead. When I eventually arrived there, I found that a huge section of the door had been chopped away. To my surprise, the sound equipment and all the ganja I stored there were still intact. The next time, I wasn't so lucky as I lost over two hundred thousand pounds worth of music, sound equipment and clothes, including master tapes and master plates of my music, which included 'World of Sorrow' by Sugar Minnott. The master tapes were priceless!

This was another big blow in what really was a world of sorrow. Suddenly, certain people I'd mingled with appeared to be more of a threat to my livelihood than the police. After the burglary in Battersea, this was déjà vu. The pain that followed the loss of an even greater collection of music and especially the loss of my recordings, was to plague me for many years, the rest didn't matter. No doubt, that experience plunged me further into deep despair and alcohol and drug addiction. I've been writing songs in between writing this autobiography and was reminded of Otis Redding by his songbook that sat next to me. In my teens, I used to tell people that he was my father, as he was my favourite singer.

I always felt as if ascended to heaven when I sang his songs with the Trax, passionately singing 'I've Been Loving You Too Long', 'Dock of the Bay' and 'Knock on Wood'. However, the first single I ever bought was 'Hey Joe' by Jimi Hendrix. I was deeply saddened by his passing, as I was by Bob Marley's later on.

The devastation I suffered from that last burglary made me wonder who my real friends were, and I questioned the much-vaunted unity of Rastafarians.

As if that wasn't enough, I was at Jah Shaka's dance in Phebes club, when a Yardie called me to the gents and demanded my ganja and money. I demanded a closer look at the gun pointing towards me and spontaneously took it out of his hand, told him that I'd left mine at home, and I'd prefer that he didn't threaten me. Instead, he should ask me for help like a brother. I then gave him back the gun and left him standing speechless. There were no witnesses. People were afraid to go to the loo when he was in there, because of his history of robbery and violence in the black community. I was victorious in that situation, only by the grace of God. I told no one of our encounter and never sought a bad-man reputation. Furthermore, I wouldn't have asked anyone to handle the situation the way I did at the time. I'm anti-guns! I believe in the demolition of all firearms. I disapprove of guns! They just lead to jail, death and devastated communities. Just like drug addiction and alcoholism.

I was asleep and unaware of that at the time, like so many men and women today. Like them, I believed I had no choice, but I did. I had my music to focus on instead. I just had to be patient, but I wasn't. It was all about riding in the fast lane, getting what I wanted, now.

That attitude was a hindrance to my music career. I saw lots of talent from the world of music and sports fall by the wayside, as drugs, alcohol, violence, immorality and dishonesty took hold. I applaud every man and woman today, regardless of age, who has enough honesty and courage to spurn such spurious glamour. All this is with hindsight, but at the time, I had the mind of an addict, which will always seek to justify negative behaviour. I didn't know that addiction is a progressive mental illness. Every time I found crack, cocaine and alcohol impossible to resist, I thought it was merely a lack of will power, but I knew something was wrong as I'd already started smashing crack pipes.

After my last trip to Jamaica, I got a luxurious flat on Stamford Hill in Cheryl's name, since I intended to get another property in my own name. She was glad to move out from her current flat for the chop marks were still there on the door from the burglary in which nothing was taken.

I had been with Angus (Drummie) from Aswad, Hughie Issachar on bass, Allan on rhythm and lead guitar, and with Winston Fergus and myself on vocals, when I was alerted about that particular incident. The sound equipment I'd acquired at that time was intended to go towards building a recording studio with a brother called Tony, who later engineered the Soul II Soul albums at his Addis Ababa Studios on the Harrow Road. Once again, my music career had been thwarted by that eighteen-month prison sentence for less than a quarter gram of ganja, causing me to miss out on the success of the Soul II Soul albums, which still sustains Tony as a landlord and businessman to this day. I wasn't living at that address when the first aborted burglary took place, but I was when the second one happened, with very unfortunate consequences.

Anyway, Cheryl was free from all that now, in a lovely flat in Stamford Hill, while I continued to live adjacent to London Fields, Hackney. It suited me best to conduct my affairs there at the time, as crack smoking began to fight for domination. I provided the funds to furnish the new flat to

Cheryl's liking, which included Regency antique furniture and six-inch white shag pile carpets.

At my flat in Eleanor Road, I entertained a range of women from Tulse Hill, Knightsbridge, Barons Court, Wood Green and so on. It's quite a sight and a heady rush when an uptown girl visits a downtown man, and I loved the experience, just as I did with any downtown girl.

Cheryl met one from South London, on a visit to that flat but said nothing at the sight of another woman in my bed. I had lived openly with her and had nothing to hide. For example, when we first met, she moved in with me, knowing that she'd be sharing living space with the mother of my second son. We were later joined by a beauty from Manchester. So, there I was, living in a flat with three lovely ladies! People wondered how I did it. I simply said that I was honest when inviting another woman to share my life with others and that having a substantial amount of money helped!

We lived harmoniously. Each woman made herself useful and my sex life was no more active than when I lived with one woman. People questioned our situation and made their remarks either for or against. I was comfortable and happy with the situation.

Eventually, the Mancunian beauty returned to Manchester, having taken my guitar without my permission. I was only pissed off about the guitar, as she was free to do as she pleased.

Rhoda was a tall, slender, beautiful, soft-spoken lady, who had a Ghanaian father and a white English mum. Rhoda left to live at her father's, before giving birth to Immanuel, whose name I chose for its meaning: 'God is with us.'

I told her to shop around for a house long before Immanuel's birth, as I was too busy making money. She never embraced the opportunity, although I assured her that we had the money. In my frustration, I underlined certain estate agents and properties in ink and asked her to call them. At the end of the day, I'd ask if she'd found anything, and was always met with a dumb look that said, what are you talking about? I never understood her reluctance to purchase a house. Surely, it was a dream come true for an expectant mother. It wasn't until many years later that I discovered that she thought the offer was a sign of rejection and feared that I was going to leave her in a house on her own with Immanuel. Ironically, she ended up living in a rented house on her own anyway. There was no way that I was going to have her and the baby live at a place where I ran my business, a flat frequented by dubious people on a daily basis. My first son's name, JaJa, meaning God's Gift, was chosen by his Aunty Beverly and myself. She's a lovely, bubbly lady, a sister with whom I spent lots of drinking sessions and happy times.

I was at Phebes nightclub at about five a.m. when a brother came running to tell me that my son had just been born at the Royal Free Hospital in Hampstead. I left the club and drove there immediately, to witness JaJa attempting to crawl out of one of those plastic incubators. That was before I started a fling with crack, cocaine and obsessive drinking. The fling turned into a love and hate relationship, which I now know was the measure of an addictive personality, and to which I would eventually become enslaved.

Brendan, my English karate expert friend, warned me of the dangers of smoking crack in the early days. He said that crack smoking was like playing Russian roulette with one's health. Not that snorting cocaine was any better, which was what he usually did! However, he couldn't watch me smoke alone and joined in after delivering this mental and physical health warning.

One day, I visited Brendan's home and got a cold reception. He angrily told me that some gunmen had been to his house and threatened him in front of his family, demanding to know my whereabouts, claiming that I had money belonging to them. He said he felt like chopping my windpipe but believed me when I declared my innocence.

Apparently, a little Rastafarian brother I knew, by the name of Judah, had received a substantial amount of ganja from them which he sold, keeping all the money for himself. He bought an ocean-going yacht and fled to the Caribbean coast in Colombia, South America, where he acquired a taste for smoking cocaine paste. He was a guy who selfishly kept a tight hold on the crack pipe after exhaling and going into a trance. It was a hell of a job to get the crack pipe from him under those conditions. He never told me about his misdeeds. Furthermore, he never mentioned how he'd told these men that he'd given me the goods before he flew to the Caribbean. I had good reasons to be paranoid, with gunmen looking for me. It wasn't a good time to be snorting coke and smoking crack.

Who these men were only came to light when Wally was released on bail and informed me that they had visited him in jail to find out my whereabouts. Straightway, I asked him to take me to their home where I declared my innocence and as a result, the matter was put to bed.

Al and his crew then decided to go the Caribbean to get their money. They succeeded easily enough, as my little friend's habit appeared to overwhelm him completely. He was a guy I had protected from bullies and that was how he repaid me. Although I was angry with him, I was relieved that the matter had been resolved. I began to see how crack smoking cracked my thinking and my relationships with others. Crack smoking is such a selfish thing! I always thought my troubles were someone else's fault, even when I was responsible.

Another acquaintance by the name of Kola, from Hampstead, warned me against cocaine use, especially smoking it, but didn't go into the details as to what the dangers were. He encouraged me to take a lot of vitamin C, which I did, thinking I had the antidote for it and therefore, no reason to stop.

I was at a shebeen one night, when a Yardie, whom I'd never met before, approached me and declared that crack and cocaine use ruins our very soul. The truth of that statement resonated within me as he walked away. I felt that God had communicated with me through him. Although I felt an impending doom, I blindly and foolishly continued down Crack Street. As that world enveloped me in darkness, I thought I was an exception to the rule, imagining I could master coke and not vice versa, although I could clearly feel that the changes it made around and within me were not for the better. The fact that I thought I could and would eventually master crack cocaine meant that it was already the master. I didn't realise it at the time but continued to treat it as if I was learning to ride an awkward bicycle.

Chapter 9
Bareback Rider

Cheryl was studying criminal law, without a care in the world as I financed everything. I encouraged her to have a line or two when she stayed up late studying for exams. I thought I was being considerate, not realising I was trying to take her hostage into my world. It amazed me how she could have one line and leave it at that. For me, that was impossible, but being an addict, it never made sense to me. She definitely wasn't an addict! I'm just glad she didn't join me in the madness.

However, she was in the grip of a different kind of madness. She was still in touch with friends of the man whom she'd had an affair with, and apparently received word that he'd passed away in a motorcycling accident.

I was about to put on my brogues one day and found them waterlogged and ruined. Photographs of my children and myself were subject to scissor cuts and I woke up one morning to find one of my locks lying next to me on the pillow. With hindsight, I'm fortunate that I woke up at all.

This was the woman I'd made plans with, to set her up with her own law firm in St Lucia. She'd been helpful when Rhoda was in maternity, bringing this and that for her, including meals and fruit.

Now Cheryl's conversation revealed how her college friends advised her against having a criminal boyfriend, as that would hinder her career. Anyway, I was ten years older than her and suddenly that became an issue. If only, she'd told me all this four years earlier. I wasn't completely surprised when I found myself locked out of the flat after returning from a trip to Jamaica. Apparently, the best time in Jamaica is Christmas and I'd turned down an invitation to stay there, only to return to calamity and chaos!

I don't know why I kept that girl. She'd already been unfaithful to me with a student at college. I told her to go but she begged me to let her stay. I relented because she'd owned up to the affair even though I was still in the dark. Then there was the incident in Grenada, and once again, I went to the rescue instead of letting her suffer the consequences of her actions when the fellow and his family ejected her from their home after she ran out of money. Life had given me opportunities to get out of that relationship and I hadn't taken them.

As a crackhead with a fragmented mind, I made fragmented decisions and entered and maintained fragmented relationships. To resolve all that meant I had to stop smoking crack. After all, I was an Ital (vegan) Rastaman, practicing complete abstinence from alcohol as well as keeping all the other Nazarite vows. Giving up crack and cocaine ought to have been a piece of cake.

I had no idea it would take so many, many years, and I'd have to fall to pieces before I let that coke and crack habit go. During that time, the thought of having sex without cocaine was out of the question. I was hooked! Bed-hopping was rife! I rode bareback and took my chances, and fortunately lived to tell the tale, only by the grace of God.

People had advised me to at least empty the flat of everything I'd bought, which would've left it completely bare. But I'm not like that, and to tell you the truth, I felt I had brought that situation on myself, by not making an exit earlier on in the relationship.

So, there I was, outside the front door, just a few days before Christmas, waiting for Cheryl to open the door. She pretended that she couldn't find her keys to get out of the flat in order to let me in. No doubt she'd stolen my keys from my hand luggage before my trip to Jamaica. As I stood there waiting, the police arrived and asked me to leave immediately, as an injunction had been lodged against me, although they refused to tell me on what grounds.

I moved into a hilltop bedsit that belonged to a prince, a friend of mine. The place was far from regal. He kept a really low profile and lived with his girlfriend elsewhere. He was an eccentric, and ran a stall selling rare comics in Brick Lane Market. He did his best to fit in downtown while his grandmother lived in Mayfair and his mother in Muswell Hill. Receiving mail on his behalf blew his cover with me when I saw HRH written in front of his name. Before that revelation, I used to empathise with his struggle to make a living.

As soon as his secret was out, I encouraged him to dress himself in a princelier manner, and not to be ashamed of his title. We have to accept the circumstances and conditions of our birth in order to maintain our sanity. He took my advice, although I'm sure that he enjoyed his downtown experience.

As crack and cocaine became more dominant in my life, I felt I had a battle on my hands. Every situation seemed a good reason to use them, including my reduced circumstances living in a bedsit. My predicament demanded more cocaine, and as a result, I went fifty-fifty on some coke I ordered.

I waited hours for it to be delivered by taxi. It still hadn't arrived when, in sheer frustration, I went out, leaving a note telling them to slip the envelope under the door.

I returned home to find an envelope outside my room! Surprised by this, I suddenly realised that the door was a tight fit, which made slipping anything but a rizla paper underneath it impossible.

Brother, I wasn't laughing, and on top of that, I had to tell my friend the bad news. It was a disappointment for him and his girlfriend. This was nothing new! Occasionally, even people I knew and trusted would sell stuff that was talcum powder. Imagine paying fifty to sixty pounds a gram for talcum powder, glucose, bicarbonate of soda or vitamin C powder!

I had to laugh at times! A big part of the buzz was the ritual of cleaning and setting up my glass pipe or pipes, then washing the coke in a laboratory test tube and seeing the coke turn to oil before it hardened like a stone, to melt and smoke on the pipe.

Lives have been devastated when a man discovered that all he got was milk powder. Again, with hindsight, these were all good reasons to quit the habit. If only it was that easy!

Suddenly, the couple in the room above were up all night listening to music. I'm sure they were having a good time at my friend's and my expense. I felt like kicking their door in and giving that guy a good hiding for stealing my stuff and having the audacity to replace it with soap powder! I had no proof, and they weren't going to admit foul play without a good hiding, so I let it ride. I didn't want to get my royal friend in trouble either.

I remember that after that disappointment, I left North London and went south to Brixton and scored more coke. I just didn't seem to care how much it was costing me financially, emotionally, socially, physically or spiritually. Deep down, I really cared about the spiritual aspect, but I was so hooked, I wanted God to help me to continue using crack, without any dire or painful consequences.

While living at the bedsit, I saw a lady who looked like someone from Vogue magazine, shopping at the local supermarket. When our eyes met on the second occasion, I discreetly handed her a note with my name and phone number that I had written at the bedsit, in hope of meeting her again.

I was confident that she'd call me, especially after seeing the look in her eyes and the smile on her face. She called me the next day! I often took her out to dinner, and even introduced her to my mother and stepfather. She introduced me to fine wines and champagne. I later discovered she was a multi-millionaire who sold the Rolls Royce and the country estate when her husband died. She settled for a small plush apartment instead and got stuck into charitable work between holiday-cruises. I thought I was going up in the world! Little did I realise, I was on my way down.

While I was with the law student Cheryl, I remember receiving an urgent and worried phone call from Mamie, telling me how she had dreamt of me falling from the sky like a stone. Her visions were always accurate. She was worried, and I was worried, but not for long. After all, the snow-queen would anaesthetise me from all my pain and transport me to a better place. Bullshit!

I bragged and boasted that I could never be really homeless. I could've stayed at a hotel like I used to do, but with my habit, I thought I'd better put up with the bedsit a little longer. I also bragged and boasted that I'd never become a slave to anyone or anything, and that I'd never be financially broke. But after that first pipe, first line, or first drink, these words became meaningless.

I didn't introduce Anne, the multi-millionaire, to cocaine. She was no stranger to it being passed around at dinner parties. She was a former dancer, one of the Bluebells, in fact. I began to see how coke and crack demolished lives and became reluctant to enter a serious relationship with any woman who had the habit. I also felt increasingly distant from the Rasta way of life. Did that have something to do with the fact that ganja had taken a back seat?

In a moment of madness, I agreed to have my locks cut off at Anne's hairdressers uptown. She booked the appointment. Among Anne's friends were lords and ladies to whom she said she'd like to introduce me. It was during that affair that I wrote 'In Your Arms', and Anne and I often toyed with the idea of performing a duet together using the songs I wrote at the time. Our relationship was fuelled with lots of champagne and wine as we drifted apart.

I soon got a ground floor flat with a basement, plus front, rear and side garden. I bought myself the biggest brass bed, 'The Emperor', from 'And So to Bed' on the Kings Road and set about furnishing the flat with quality purchases. I was involved in all sorts of deals at the time and found myself struggling to put business before pleasure. I became increasingly aware of how influential crack had become in my life and went about smashing crack pipes more regularly. That meant equally regular trips to the cocaine paraphernalia shops in Camden Town, Kensington or wherever!

I bought two Doberman pups from a man I called Aeroplane Joe and named them Solomon and Sheba. I fed them on cuts I bought and boiled from the butcher and with fresh herrings from the fishmongers. I also maintained all the health checks they needed and was surprised to find that vets were just as expensive as doctors.

I had this terribly empty feeling inside and felt like I was going nowhere, although I was making lots of money. I had to have bags of cocaine near me, as I was always afraid of running out. I kept a stash in the basement with a substantial amount of cash. I was in pain and Mamie's vision haunted me.

I went to answer my doorbell one day, wondering who could that be, and lo and behold, it was Cheryl. I remembered the saying, "give an inch and they'll take a mile", and instantly told her to leave my front door, without asking her to explain how she found my address. I used the f-word, which I rarely ever used in my vocabulary.

I recall the day when I left the flat I shared with her to go and visit Wally. I was set upon by several men from Customs and Excise, just as I went to press the doorbell. They ushered me into the house and insisted that I keep quiet. I heard my friend's girlfriend crying in despair and denial, as I stood in the hallway, where I was searched down to my underwear. I didn't hear my friend's voice at all. As I had no drugs on me and only had fifty pounds in cash, I assumed that they'd let me go. Instead, I was detained for another twenty-four hours, throughout which I was questioned regarding coke dealing. "We only smoke ganja together," was the bewildered response, and I left it at that.

On my release, I shot across to Knightsbridge to smoke crack with an elegant beauty called Bubbles, in an apartment opposite Harrods. My paranoia grew and kept growing, as I believed I was being followed by Customs and Excise. I was at my new flat when I received the unbelievable news that my friend had been sentenced to twenty-four years. That sentence was felt like the tremors of an earthquake amongst the criminal fraternity. But that couldn't stop me from smoking crack! It was a reason to smoke even harder. There were lots of people who frowned at crack smokers and dealers and gave them bad press. However, the number of smokers and dealers kept growing. Many of the anti-crack brigade eventually came out as users, closet smokers or dealers.

Chapter 10

In the House of the Kray Twins – This Way Madness Lies

No 1 Evering Road was a house that once belonged to the Kray Twins, a lovely elderly lady told me when she asked me if I knew about the previous owners and said I didn't know. I'd just moved in and was eager to furnish the place to my liking.

Next thing I knew, a girl called Julie, with whom I had a one-night fling on the floor of her flat, rang my doorbell and asked me if she could stay for a week or two, until she found a place of her own. Reluctantly, I said yes, on condition that it was for no more than two weeks. Six weeks later, she was still there. I wasn't going to let her cramp my style, and carried on bed-hopping, seeking to fill a void within that could never be filled.

Then there was the inner conflict between my way of life and my desire to make music. Perhaps I should have said my way of death at the time, as Alcohol Avenue and Crack Cocaine Street were awash with news concerning deaths or car crashes where limbs were lost. My reaction to such news was to smoke more crack. I began to drink alcohol more heavily at that time, as I found it smoothed the rough edges from crack and cocaine use and made my descent from any high smoother and more manageable, or so I thought.

In short, since I had that fling with Julie, she'd turned from being a straight girl, who worked for an airline, into a gangster's moll, with good connections. In our relationship, money flowed like water as my pain grew greater. I felt empty and alone, no matter how many people were around.

I noticed Solomon and Sheba were up all night, barking until dawn. It pissed me off because it disturbed my crack smoking. As a result, I stopped handling crack and cocaine in the kitchen, where they slept as puppies at the time. With no more crumbs of crack or coke powder to lick off of the kitchen tiles, the barking ceased forthwith.

I also turned down many requests from Julie to join me in the habit. Julie and I spent lots of time shopping and eating out. We also took my five children out on lovely trips to lovely places. I clearly remember us enjoying a picnic under the shade of a big tree, with sunshine and blue skies.

At my house, I forbade the children to enter the kitchen while I medicated. However, it was all in vain. My eldest son, JaJa, entered that kitchen one day, mouth gaping, beady eyed, as he beheld me with Bunsen burner ablaze and glass pipe filled with smoke, as I sucked my poison from the bubbling water. Before I exhaled, I gave him one angry look, at which point he made an instant about-turn, exiting through the door which I indicated with crack pipe in hand. I was instantly riddled with guilt, shame, regret and remorse, but my reaction was to smoke harder.

I warned Julie that both of us smoking crack would result in the demise of our relationship. Her pursuit of the glass pipe was relentless, and in order to avoid any further interruptions of my trips to the twilight zone, I gave in to her wishes.

After her first pipe, she grew steadily greedier and more selfish, demanding another pipe, with complete disregard for whose turn it was, as if I was only there to serve like a bartender. Although I bought her a pipe, I kept control of the crack and cocaine. Her avarice was so ugly that it disgusted me. When her eyes turned from blue to green after exhalation, I felt as if I was in the presence of the devil. I needed her to leave, but she constantly avoided my insinuations. After a while, I noticed my coke stash was short in weight every time I went to reload for another session. Soon, I discovered that my money I stashed in the basement was also shrinking by exactly the same amount, on a daily basis.

Julie denied everything and was deaf and dumb when I asked her about the roll-up on the floor and the wet patch on my brand-new mattress. Her deaf and dumb posturing turned into ridicule when she said it was all in my imagination. The mattress was on the floor as I waited for the rest of the bed to arrive. I picked up the roll-up that laid next to the mattress, put it in her hand and asked, "Is this my imagination?" I took her hand and pressed it on the wet patch on the mattress and asked her again, "Is this my imagination?" She became deaf and dumb all over again, and my requests for her to leave immediately fell on deaf ears. I didn't smoke cigarettes or roll-ups at the time. And the audacity of her sexually entertaining someone on my bed, in my flat, together with everything else that went missing on a daily basis, meant that she had to go.

Then there was the incident when I discovered that the crack that I was sharing with her at the table somehow managed to find itself lodged inside her bra and her knickers.

In fact, the crack was disappearing so fast from the table that I was only managing to get one pipe at a time, no matter how much I put down. It was my crack, bought with my money, and I refused to give her anymore while she continued to deny everything. She was free to go and buy her own. Instead she took offence, smashed the crack pipe and cut and slashed at me with the broken glass, her hand bleeding as it cut into her grip. She felt no pain as she cut and slashed at me again and again. I held her until she became exhausted, choosing not to fight back, in case I did something I'd regret later.

That incident was soon followed by Julie lunging at me with my longest and largest kitchen knife. I ran from the kitchen into the sitting room on that occasion and held the door fast after shutting it. Julie stabbed repeatedly at the door, then began thrusting and slashing at my feet through the gap under the door as I held it shut. She had to go!

I arrived home one evening and another check on my stash and money revealed exactly the same losses again. This had been going on for six weeks. I heard her say, "Hello darling" from the bathroom. I was in a seriously angry mood and didn't waste my breath responding or asking her why my scales kept repeating the same story or since when had money grown legs. Instead, I held her head underwater in the bath, her eyes staring up at me through the water. They got wider and wider as her face changed colour. I held her there firmly, despite all her splashing and kicking in her efforts to free herself. Her hands fought back in vain, as I crouched over her, gripping her throat like a vice, while staring into her eyes that bulged with horror. I held her there until she started to drink water. Then, I released her.

I calmly asked her to leave, while she coughed and spluttered in fear and disbelief at what had just happened to her and insisted that all her belongings went with her. I changed my wet clothes and left the building, coldly reminding her that she'd better be absent by the time I return from the night-club. I got back at about midday the following day. Julie had disappeared with all her belongings and had taken my two puppies as well as the large stash of sensimilla that I stored in the veg section in the fridge. I took my losses with a smile of relief. She'd had her last pay day.

However, days later, on returning home from certain escapades involving crack cocaine and alcoholic activities, I noticed my pot plants had been knocked over. Someone had entered my flat and this wasn't my imagination or paranoia. She'd returned my keys but obviously had a spare set. I immediately put a stop to that by getting every lock changed. With Julie out of the way, I felt like celebrating, and the only way I knew how was to warm up the crack pipe. I was free from her, but not free from the loneliness, pain and paranoia that are all parts of a larger fear. At the time, I thought I was untouchable, and that I would eventually master these symptoms of inordinate drug abuse.

Freddie the gangster, with his Yardie and African connections, paid me a visit to reveal how Julie had tried to sabotage our business together by telling them that I was not to be trusted. He continued by saying that no woman could ruin our friendship, for we went back a long way. I assured him and the African gangster boss, called Bola, that I no longer slept with the enemy, and she'd never ever enter my house again. They were surprised that I'd tolerated such a catalogue of financial losses and disrespect for so long.

Another gangster friend of mine by the name of PJ accompanied me to my house after the club. We both had a woman in tow. He occupied the sitting-room while I was engaged in the bedroom. I found myself going out to buy more champagne at eleven a.m., after getting home at nine a.m. It was unlike me to purchase alcohol for consumption so early in the day. I thought about it, then washed it out of my mind with the first swig, as I attended to business with my temporary lover.

I thought plenty of champagne, cognac, cocaine, crack, sensimilla and women were a heavenly combination. I noticed sensimilla had slipped from number one to number two, as the snow-queen dominated the number one spot. I'd believed that sensimilla's reign at the number one spot would be for life. This change in events perturbed me, but once again, I swiftly went into denial. There was no way that crack, cocaine, alcohol and money could replace the love of a woman in my life.

PJ had become notorious for giving Ranking Dread, a Yardie gang-leader, a good hiding on the frontline at Sandringham Road Hackney E8, as he refused to be intimidated by the guy's reputation. After all, this was our patch, where we grew up as schoolchildren. We'd been on missions together in our quest to survive and enjoy ourselves as teenagers, and I was proud of him for sending out a message that we were not to be bullied on our turf. PJ and I gave the women a really good time, and they reciprocated. Like Freddie, PJ knew me from primary school days. We had an altercation once that started in a laundrette, spilled onto the pavement, and ended around the corner. We were little boys in our first year of secondary school in which I was victorious then, and that episode was water under the bridge, as we grew to be good friends. PJ had gotten himself a basement club and swapped me a Bang and Olufsen Hi-Fi system for the huge bass and midrange speaker boxes I had intended to use in the music business. The boxes sounded sweet in his club.

I thought of Wally, another gangster figure and close friend, who'd received twenty-four years for cocaine importation. I was still at the flat that I'd shared with Julie, as

I recalled the days when we walked the streets together, determined not to return home without any money. We always managed that somehow. But in all honesty, I was always the engineer and driving force on these numerable expeditions and gave him half the money, although others would say that he didn't deserve such generosity for simply tagging along. Furthermore, I was the one who gave his ex-wife money while he was in prison, although he never did the same for me, except on two occasions when he gave me five hundred pounds and three hundred pounds respectively. On top of all that, I also invested my energy, time and money in him and got Sir Fray to do the same and was only repaid the money that we invested and never received a share of the profits that followed. After all, this was a so-called friend who didn't respond to my letter asking for financial help when I was in rehab and was instrumental in causing others to burgle my home although he denied any implication when I questioned him. God only knows why I endured his dishonesty, selfishness and disrespect for so long.

The Mendy brothers were charismatic friends of mine from the same mould. They were connected to the boxing world and got themselves a world-champion in the form of Nigel Benn. I knew their sister, Nina, the matriarch of the family. She spent lots of time with us at the squat where Sir Fray stored and played his sound system, along with ganja dealing, smoking, heavy drinking and partying. I knew many shady characters from East, West, North and South London and neighbouring counties but I also knew many honest and hardworking people.

I remembered Maverick and his younger brother, Tabby the Alley Cat, who used to tag along with us to the Ilford Palais, Whiskey A-Go-Go, The Flamingo, Ronnie Scotts, Night Angel, the Roaring Twenties, and other clubs. The Alley Cat, also known as Dennis Andries, eventually became a world boxing champion and I deeply admired and respected his self-discipline, which included road running, no drinking or smoking, and complete honesty.

Maverick was also an honest man like our other mutual friend, Bishop, with whom we also frequented the West End clubs in our early and late teens. Maverick and Bishop would get drunk on one little bottle of Babycham or Cherry B and you'd better watch out if they had two. I found that baffling but wished at the same time that I could get drunk on such a minute intake of alcohol, as this would've saved me lots of money that I could've spent elsewhere. I didn't know it then, but Maverick, almost the virtual teetotaller, descended into alcoholism and is no longer with us today. He was a jovial and natty dresser and I can hear his laughter with fondness as I write these words. There wasn't a dull moment with Maverick as he produced one joke after another. "God bless you Maverick!"

His beautiful mother is still here with us as I write this book. Although I didn't see her the last time I called at her home, I trust I will the next time I pay her a visit. As for the Alley Cat, it was a pleasure to see him again, when we met by chance at Clapton Pond, after the passage of so many years. That meeting resulted in both of us paying PJ a visit.

I remembered another occasion with Wally, when we visited an acquaintance after scoring some coke, which we washed at his home. We washed enough to last us a while only to discover that we were only getting one or two pipes when we ought to be getting more. We looked at each other questioningly and washed more, only to end up with the same result. We knew that Tricky Dicky was stealing the rocks that we came to share with him but couldn't catch him at it at the table. This frustrating, annoying and disrespectful situation caused us to decide to leave prematurely. Before I left, I used the loo, only to discover the lost rocks under a roll of tissue paper. Pleasantly surprised, I pocketed them and told Wally of my discovery after we left. He didn't want any of it, so I smoked it all as soon as I got home. Incidents like that made me think that I was better than people like Tricky Dickey.

After all, I had the same habit and didn't notice how my relationship with my children was waxing and waning, whereas, once upon a time, it was as solid as a rock. Despite all my good intentions in my relationships with the snow-queen, I was the one who was being overwhelmed, and I didn't like it. But oblivious to the cost, I was determined to master her rather than let her go. I was the one with the brains, the eyes, the ears, the mouth, the hands, legs, feet and spirit. Therefore, I would have dominion over the white powder. I thought that the more I danced with her, the more inevitable that dominion would be.

My insanity counselled me that to run away from the snow-queen would be a sign of weakness. After all, others appeared to be managing okay with her! Little did I realise that they were all drowning one way or another with that stuff.

I missed my friend Wally and saw how crack had damaged our brotherly relationship. One time, I called at his place and getting no response, I went round to the back to find the bathroom light on. Straight away, I knew he was lost in there with the pipe. This had never happened before. We could always call each other at any hour, confident that the door would always be opened. The crack habit changed the dynamics of all that. I wanted my old friend back. I wanted my old self back. I didn't realise how impossible that would be, unless I broke my engagement with the snow-queen. I remembered those West End hotels where Wally and I stayed under fictitious names with our girlfriends. I recalled travelling to Newport and Cardiff with Suzanne, Wally and Rita, filled with a zest for life.

On one occasion, I slapped a man in the face, at a house party in Newport. I slapped him for refusing to accept the answer "no" from my girlfriend Suzanne, who became weary of his unwanted advances.

It transpired that this guy was a local gang leader and knowing this, Wally rushed to the kitchen and armed himself with a large knife, just in case the place exploded in all-out war. Quite inexplicably, the opposite happened. We ran out of money in Newport and Wally paid for our meals with one gold bracelet and used another to borrow some money, for our train fare back to London. Those were the good old days of learning in the University of Life, on the streets of Great Britain. Lots of reggae stars visited Wally's home and mine as we went through our ups and downs. I missed Solomon and Sheba.

Chapter 11
Happy Families

There I was, in a new flat, waiting for the rest of my big brass bed to arrive. I'd only received the base and mattress so far. Sitting there amid the emptiness, I decided I must change. I had to find the right woman, someone who didn't smoke crack, snort coke or drink heavily. How could I expect to find a girl like that at a night-club, especially during the weekdays?

I was in no hurry to replace Solomon and Sheba. I realised that I'd left them in the kitchen on their own for far too long and far too often, while I toured the city of London. I used to feel as if I was king alongside my snow-queen, a man for whom every door he knocked upon opened and became his home, for as long as he had her with him. Although I left enough meat and frozen raw herring to thaw out, knowing it would last Solomon and Sheba at least a few days, with enough water as well, I knew it wasn't right. I wasn't going to put any dogs through that again. I believed the solution was in finding a loving and loyal woman, thinking that would make me whole again.

Little did I realise that I was already complete, and to think I was half a person was handing my power over to someone else. In retrospect, it's painfully apparent that I was setting myself up for disappointments in relationships. I didn't realise that addiction to drugs and alcohol was consuming me, and that I wouldn't kick the habit for any woman at all.

A notorious acquaintance, by the name of Glen nicknamed James Bond, came to see me with his girlfriend in tow. I was surprised to find him requesting a loan as I had heard that his girlfriend was a rich and generous lady.

Sometime later, when I went to collect the debt as agreed, the woman broke down in tears, saying that she had no money and that Glen had moved out to live with a beautiful blonde in South London.

Filled with compassion, I assured her that she had nothing to worry about. I felt for her and her three children. After making myself at home with a few lines and some bottles of Bollinger, it became apparent to me that her cupboards and fridge were bare. As night turned to day, I discovered builders were calling for money owed, and the bank was in the process of repossessing the property. I couldn't believe a woman would put herself and her children in such a position to support a man's crack habit, especially when she didn't share his predilection.

Believing this devastating experience had caused her to change her attitude, I paid off more debts than I care to remember and helped to save the house from repossession in the process. By that time, I no longer had the businesses I'd invested in earlier. My life was dedicated to smoking crack instead of business.

I don't actually recall her or her teenaged children: Jason, Simone and Anthony, ever showing any appreciation for what I'd done for them in a few short weeks. Then I had a bright idea! If I got married, the dynamics in my life would change, I'd slow down and control my crack use. Michelle didn't smoke or drink, and I presumed that would help. Furthermore, I assumed that marrying Michelle would prove to her children that I was nothing like Glen, who beat and bullied their mother for money and crack and left them on the verge of homelessness and hunger.

I'd been in the house for some weeks, just smoking crack, snorting cocaine and drinking champagne. My life was standing still but I noticed my money was shrinking faster than I was spending. I began to doubt Michelle's honesty but said nothing. A little later, I discovered that Jason was a burglar with a coke habit, apparently triggered by him dabbling with Glen's white stuff during his stay there.

Whilst in bed, I asked Michelle if she'd consider changing her surname. I wasn't in a hurry, but she insisted that I marry her now or never. I told her that my pending court case, for which I was signing on at Hendon Police Station whilst on bail, might result in a custodial sentence. "I'll stand by you if you marry me, but can't guarantee it if you don't," was Michelle's reply. I was so impressed with her response that I decided to proceed with this matrimonial venture.

Admittedly, there was some reluctance even as I went ahead, bought rings and arranged a date for the civil wedding. We ordered a couple of minicabs and invited some friends and family at short notice. We asked an acquaintance to leave the car repairs he was making and join us as best man. We even managed to order crates of champagne and flowers en-route to the registry office!

This was done in between drinking and smoking crack. All my decisions and actions were influenced by these substances, and I was expecting a good outcome as a result. Unfortunately, at such short notice, hardly anyone invited turned up, including Michelle's two sons. A handful of people, including JaJa's mum Peggy, our minicab driver, the best man, Michelle's mother, Lila and a few others attended the reception at the marital home. Michelle and her mum argued, about what I don't know. She resented her mother, claiming she was jealous of her and hadn't played any part in her life and upbringing. She put this down to the fact that she was an adopted child. Nonetheless, I urged her to make peace with her mum.

At one stage, I noticed Michelle crying in the kitchen, and thought she was shedding tears of happiness, only to hear her say that she still cared about Glen and would help him if she could. I realised there and then that I'd made a big mistake. I was about to leave the house and turn my back on the marriage. However, I decided to delay it for a month or two just to be absolutely sure and then leave. There was also that people pleasing side of me that didn't want to upset anyone at the reception. As far as I was concerned, Michelle definitely wasn't in love with me. I felt that she'd used me to make her ex-boyfriend jealous.

Within a month, insults were already being hurled at me. Shortly thereafter, I decided to tell her that I was returning to my flat. I was about to speak when Michelle spoke first, revealing that she was pregnant. I felt obliged to stay and to meet my responsibilities as a father. I was determined to do better than I did with my other five children and their two mothers. I didn't let Michelle know my true feelings. I felt trapped in a loveless marriage. As a result, my relationship with the snow-queen grew more compulsive and obsessive. My alcohol consumption rose rapidly, and I began drinking in pubs to avoid the disrespect I was experiencing from Michelle and her twins, in particular.

I found out that they were angry with me for not including them in my decision to marry their mother. They felt that I'd taken over their home, and far too quickly. They were right about that! But after witnessing the way their mum had been abused by Glen, I was appalled by their behaviour, as I showed more interest in their welfare and education than their mother did.

Michelle told me that she didn't know how to raise children as she was never raised by her parents. She was a fostered child from birth. I thought that was a feeble excuse. The house was attractive on the outside, and luxurious on the inside, and to outsiders, it seemed as if we were living a dream life. On the contrary, I felt that I was the unhappiest man on the planet. I had acquired more pain in my search for joy. I always believed in having alternative accommodation and that didn't change after I got married.

Eventually, however, I rented out my flat at Michelle's request. I did so hoping that it would help to improve our relationship. I wondered about the wisdom of living with a woman with children, when I already had children with two other women whom I didn't live with. I didn't go for co-habiting with women who had children from other men, and now, suddenly, I found myself married to one, six weeks after we met.

As Michelle relaxed into pregnancy, I attended to my responsibilities and my rights as best as I could, my right being drinking and drugging. Even the house phone was cut off and wasn't reconnected until I paid twelve hundred pounds for something that had nothing to do with me. So, when Michelle asked me to pay her bank overdrafts for debts incurred through crack addiction, I wasn't surprised. "No!" was my reply.

Suddenly, my cashmere cardigans went missing along with my brand-new shoes from Church's and Russell and Bromley, and most of my ganja went for a walk as well. Not all on the same day, mind you. I found a couple of kilos of sensimilla and my shoes in the dustbin on separate occasions, just before the dustmen were due to collect the rubbish. I later discovered that Simone was wearing my cardigans to school. Although she didn't ask for my permission to go into my wardrobe and take them, I didn't mind. But finding my ganja and brand-new shoes in the dustbin really upset me.

I figured I'd spent over one hundred thousand pounds on that house within six months, and there were these teenagers being hostile towards me. They never answered me when I said, "Good morning", nor displayed any willingness to engage in any conversation whatsoever. The twins eventually got Anthony to join the rebellion, and Michelle was on their side, whether they were right or not. She also continued to unleash her daily tirade of abuse in my direction, until I began to wonder what kind of home Nathan and Leah would be born into.

Some of my friends were made to feel so unwelcome by Michelle and the twins that I chose to meet them in the pub instead. I hated pubs, and there I was sitting in them for hours, buying mostly draught Guinness. I was frustrated, angry and in pain, but I tried not to show it. I did my best to make sure Michelle relaxed during her pregnancy. My drinking habits increased, and I left my crack smoking until after everyone had gone to bed. I observed that all three teenagers basically lived in their rooms and only came out to the kitchen and bathroom when it was necessary. We lived like strangers in that house. The teenage twins were also venomous and angry in their limited conversations with their mother.

So here we were, a houseful of angry strangers, and I felt like I was the only one trying to be friends. I also had to make sure that I kept my wallet secure, as I caught Jason one night in the bedroom, searching my clothes for money while I pretended to be asleep. He was a prolific burglar, registered at a school he didn't attend. When I asked the headmaster about Jason's attendance record, he simply replied, "What do you want me to do? Keep him on a ball and chain?" His headmaster wasn't interested, and neither was Michelle.

I often went to police stations, sometimes at four or five a.m., and even pleaded with the youth court for his release on a few occasions. One time, the police came to the house to arrest him on suspicion of stealing thirty thousand pounds from a briefcase left in a car. I told them Jason had been with me at the time of the offence, which was true. I also assured them that Jason would be going everywhere with me for the foreseeable future, as I was fed up with multiple court appearances and visits to various police stations.

Everywhere I went, I took Jason with me, a situation that lasted for about one month. I established a rapport with him and discovered that he loved his mum, but hated her for putting her boyfriends first, before Simone, Anthony and himself. Although their mum had always given them more pocket money than most children and bought them whatever they fancied, they all missed spending quality time with her. Michelle thought that money could buy you love. Well, here I was, doing the same thing, financing everything and expecting love in return.

The pain increased as I neither saw, heard, nor felt love from anyone in that house. I began to feel for my other children, who saw less of me and had less money spent on them. They came to stay at the house as often as possible. It was a strained affair, as they received frosty receptions from Jason, Simone and Anthony. I did my best to assure the stepchildren that my children were only visitors and to be hospitable, not hostile. Michelle refused to discuss anything. In fact, she never had time to sit down and have a heart-to-heart conversation.

I had hoped to resurrect my music career in a happy marriage, but constant turmoil made this impossible. Meanwhile, my drinking and crack smoking grew, as I found myself making acquaintances at the pubs I frequented, when

I became reluctant to go home. "You're not a black man! Your friends are plonkers!" Michelle would scream. She criticised the way I ate, drank and smoked crack, the way I ran my business, and even taunted me about my mother being too middle class and so on. It reminded me of living with my father, without the physical abuse that followed. Instead, these beatings were essentially mental and emotional in nature.

The pub bell for last orders reminded me of the school bell I had so hated when it rang for home time. A dark cloud gathered over me at such moments. I'd never experienced such a dislike for any house I had lived in since my childhood. To be reliving such an experience, after all these years, was unbelievable and excruciating.

I felt so ashamed of the sham marriage that my pride wouldn't allow me to discuss it with my friends or family. I sat in pubs instead, angry and awash with self-pity.

Chapter 12

Tagg's Island

I remember my delight at leaving 27 Priory Road for a month. It was unforgettable. I was out of range of the verbal bullets that Michelle launched at me.

Italian Tony, the fraudster; Dodge, the ex-army hard man; Bob, the esoteric intellectual; and I, agreed to go to Tagg's Island to decorate Benny's two-storey luxury houseboat. Tony was later unable to go with us, for some reason that I cannot recall.

Benny traded in mountains of assorted commodities, ranging from sugar to gold. He was also highly respected amongst the criminal fraternity and used the services of ex-soldiers to recoup money owed to him.

He let us his two bed-roomed houseboat, next to his home. I accompanied him to Tesco's, where his generosity assured that our cupboards were fully stocked. He pointed out that we'd find all the alcohol we needed in the studio flat, purposely built to house his cat. It was fully furnished, with shag pile carpeting, sofa, fridge, cooker, TV, telephone and all mod-cons, including double glazed patio doors. That little studio flat sat on the land behind our bungalow, while our house and Benny's two-storey beauty sat on the Thames, chained to the riverbank. Both had a veranda, giving us access to the boats on the river.

Dodge did his fishing from our veranda. I was surprised to discover that his fishing rods were worth more than many cars on the road. As a keen fisherman, he'd return to check his bait after work on Benny's home or after a session at the Cardinal Wolsey pub. We had to go through quaint and winding narrow lanes, embellished with lovely houses that resembled holiday homes, then cross a narrow bridge that connected us to the mainland, and traverse the main road that took us to the pub in Hampton Court.

That's where I met Norman, who chose to drink with me instead of Bob and Dodge. I was on his wavelength. He was going through a troubled marriage, drank copious amounts of champagne from noon till night, laughing and joking, as he spent some of his daily winnings from horse racing. His tips came from a reliable source.

We extended our drinking at his house one night, in the absence of his wife and son. Norman hoped that they would return one day, but they never did. For the first time, I found myself unable to finish a bottle of the best and most potent vintage red I had ever tasted. I was enveloped in a cloudy mist after the second glass, lost track or interest in our conversation, as oblivion beckoned. As soon as I was able, I gratefully made my exit to the guest room.

Nonetheless, I felt Norman's pain and desperation to save his marriage, as we talked over the breakfast that he'd prepared. I listened intently, without revealing the similarities to my marriage at the time. The fact that he ran a successful construction business meant that he could consume entire crates of champagne stockpiled behind the bar.

I enjoyed admiring the curves of the ladies in riding britches as they entered the pub and made their way into the glorious sunshine in the pub garden, which ran down to the river.

I felt so at home in the area, I wanted to move in. I also experienced a deep and satisfying sleep on the houseboat that made me feel refreshed and energised in the morning. I wondered why. Then, late one night on the verge of sleep, I became conscious of the houseboat gently rocking on the river and realised that that was the answer.

I found myself drinking alcohol earlier than usual, as Bob and Dodge opened cans of Tennent's Super at breakfast, at around seven thirty a.m. I joined in, although I hated the taste and smell of the stuff. Somehow, I still liked the effect, and remained completely oblivious to the fact that I was descending into alcoholism.

Dodge would carry on drinking long after Bob and I had retired. I questioned him about it one day, wishing I could carry on drinking as he did, without cocaine to back it up.

I changed my mind when he told me about some of the horrors of war. The slaughter of innocent and defenceless village people, in faraway places. Then, there were the barmy orders from certain army officers that led to the unnecessary deaths of brothers in arms. I never asked him for the names of the wars or of their locations. He was a very haunted man.

Benny and Serena wanted the interiors of every room painted in pink beige, from top to bottom. Somehow, we managed to do a good day's work with alcohol in our system. Benny, his lovely wife Serena, their two dogs and a cat, were a class act, and we had to produce work of the highest standard.

During a break, Benny asked us to lower the volume of the music late at nights, as the sounds of Bob Marley and the Wailers disturbed the neighbours. I wondered if they would have complained had it been Beethoven.

Needless to say, I was reluctant to leave when the time came and intended to return as soon as I could for a rented stay at the property, although I was welcome to stay without cost. Life on Tagg's Island was like being on a holiday. We all thanked Benny and Serena for their hospitality.

Dodge and I split company with Bob on our return to London. As we proceeded on our journey, two men walked past, making racist remarks aimed at me. Well! Dodge, the white ex-army hard man, flourished a bayonet I had never seen him with before, and chased the would-be warmongers away, with an avalanche of derogatory remarks. As Dodge's blade advanced and flashed under the streetlights, our adversaries showed us a clean pair of heels. No matter how fast we ran, they ran even faster. Dodge was so fired up, he surprised me by running faster than I did. When I retired, he kept on going, until he realised the futility of the chase.

With pen in hand, I remembered Dodge's words: "My dad always said that, 'To work with black people, is to be lucky!'" Well, he certainly invested in his luck on that occasion.

Unfortunately, many months later, I gave Dodge a good hiding on the night I sought revenge for being attacked, outside the Queen's Pub in Crouch End. He wasn't part of the crew that had attacked me, and had he been there, I don't think it would have happened. So, Dodge, wherever you are, I humbly ask for your forgiveness.

Dodge had gotten rich from tons of marijuana smuggled into this country when he was in the army. The colonel got whiff of their plans, and confiscated about two tons of ganja, leaving Dodge and the crew about the same amount. Very generous indeed! Dodge had used the proceeds to buy land, which he let out to farmers, and showed me the deeds to prove it. However, his drinking took its toll, as he coughed and peed blood. He was the haunted man of war, who left the city to retire in the southwest of England, to indulge in his favourite pastime at the sea. I'd like to think that Dodge is recovering from the mental and emotional scars of war and alcoholism, wherever he is.

As for intellectual Bob, apart from being into esoteric things, he was a great chef. He eventually disappeared when he received an inheritance that allowed him to buy a boathouse on the Thames. I have no doubt that Bob and Italian Tony were alcoholics as well. With hindsight, I see how alcoholics gravitate towards each other, reinforcing each other's drinking.

Chapter 13

From Cala D'or
to Meltdown

As the delivery date for the twins drew close, I hoped that their arrival would cement us together as a family. I had made arrangements to go to Jamaica, just before Michelle was admitted into the maternity ward, but cancelled when I realised the twins were due in days. She insisted that I go!

I stayed one night in a Kingston Hotel, then caught a cab to Negril, where I stayed at a five-star hotel owned by the family of a friend. I had discussed the music business with him and how many reggae artists we were going to get to play in London and the rest of England. I found it easy to abstain from crack out there and stuck to smoking sensi and indica. I'd wake up early in the morning, jog on the beach, have a sea bath, eat some roasted breadfruit, fried plantain and calalloo at the art and craft village, then return to my hotel and rinse off in the shower.

I enjoyed the Negril nightlife with a brother, the owner of the hotel, and bought a fine piece of wood carving from a vendor on the beach. I was offered opportunities to smuggle ganja, in an ingenious way. However, I'd learnt that all that glitters is not gold. I kept the discipline and focused on the music business I had to attend to.

I thought of Michelle and the babies and kept in touch by phone. I was still in Jamaica when they were born. From Negril, I flew to Kingston, for a meeting at the Pegasus Hotel. The flight cost only a quarter of what I spent on a cab fare, returning from Kingston to Negril. Furthermore, the cab was far from roadworthy, with no window wipers and faults all-over. It was amazing how they kept those vehicles on the road. I was glad to pay the inflated cab fare, hoping it would help in some way. I returned to Negril and had run out of time to visit Sir Fray, who had resettled in Jamaica, with a hotel in Montego Bay.

Then, I returned to England, looking forward to meeting the twins. It was a great relief to know that they had arrived in good health. I bought them the best cot, baby clothes, sheets, blankets and the best pram they had at Peter Jones, on my way to the house from the airport. Again, I hoped that the arrival of Nathan and Leah would turn that house into a home. My heart melted at first sight of their innocence and beauty. Their room had already been transformed into a baby room, the day they came home from the maternity ward. After missing out on living with my other children, I was determined to stick around and meet my responsibilities.

Yet deep within, I felt that this would only be possible with a change in Michelle's attitude towards me and most of my friends. This gave me a sinking feeling and another reason to drink and drug, amidst the joy I felt at the birth of my children. All the bottle making and nappy changing skills that I had learned at the age of seven, came in very handy indeed. I was glad that Michelle chose to breastfeed, but that only lasted a few weeks, as she said she found breastfeeding hard work.

As for me, I still frequented night-clubs. I'd return to the house at five, six, seven a.m., attend to the twins as soon as they woke up and be out wheeling them in the park at the rear of our house by nine a.m. We made good use of the swings in the park, as soon as they were big and strong enough.

I'm grateful for the experience of being awakened by the twins, as they crept into our bed and made their loving and needy presence felt at first light. I'm grateful for the mentally and physically exhausting process of raising babies and appreciate the role of mothers everywhere. I wanted to refer to the house as my marital home, but I still didn't feel at ease.

Michelle and the stepchildren's attitude towards me seemed to be getting worse instead of better. We had a cleaner and nanny by the name of Gloria, and someone else to do the ironing. Gloria came on the scene when Michelle decided to return to managing properties for a Jewish man in the West End offering services in dominatrix, about three months after giving birth.

After a while, I felt as if all the anger and frustration my stepchildren felt towards their mum, was being redirected at me, as I made good target practice. Michelle must have been relieved to have me in the line of fire, taking much of the heat away from her. Maybe that's why she never asserted herself. Being in love with me would've helped.

Our weekends revolved around the twins, taking them out shopping, to the park, swings and other infant activities, in the area of Crouch End. I was disappointed that the stepchildren didn't play a more supporting role regarding Nathan and Leah. At the time, it seemed as if they loved them from a distance, although we shared the same roof. Apart from sex, the only other times Michelle and I connected was in buying gifts for each other. We had fleeting moments of happiness, with her cooking while I played the music that we both liked, including reggae, jazz and soul. She was a great jazz fan!

As my alcoholic consumption increased, I'd hire a cab for the day, to take us to Thorpe Park and back. The other three siblings stayed behind. When I went shopping, I'd buy something for everyone, and occasionally took Jason with me, to choose whatever he liked. On many occasions, I'd ask Michelle for a heart-to-heart discussion, but she was always too tired, or too busy. We never ever watched the TV or a film together, as a married couple. I took to gardening and loved it. In fact, I found it very therapeutic. Attending to the twins was a joy, a privilege, and an unforgettable experience, although very tiring. Michelle was so exhausted that when Nathan and Leah were six to nine months old, she went on holiday to Majorca, with her good friend Lana.

I was left to my own devices, and mixed cloak and dagger business with drinking, and crack smoking. I lacked inspiration to write songs, unless it was the blues. I was anxious to write upbeat stuff at the time and needed upbeat experiences to help me. Michelle called me a week later in distress, said her friend had returned to London, and that she needed my support. I was making a lot of money at the time and thought, what timing! Well, I dropped everything, and found myself in Majorca the next day.

I was a vegan on the flight but got drunk on the plane and headed straight to the bar and barbecue on arrival. The next thing I knew, I was eating barbecued steak. My vegan days were over! Looking on the bright side, I thought having the same diet as Michelle might bring us closer together. She had complained and taunted me about me being a vegan and the difficulty of having to cook separate meals instead of one menu for all the family. She certainly didn't say that before we were married.

Michelle was surprised, and happy to see me eating meat. However, I felt that I'd lost some of myself, after reverting to it in a blackout. I could've returned to my Ital ways but carried on devouring flesh in a desperate bid to save our marriage, so that I could be there for the twins. For me, it was all about the twins, or else, I would have left ages ago.

For some reason, Michelle and I got on really well. We worked joyfully and harmoniously with our babies in this relaxed and sunny setting, away from Jason, Simone and Anthony, even though I missed them. Surprisingly, there were no tongue lashings from Michelle. For a moment, we were living in a different and better world. We explored the island, admiring the beauty of the landscape and its people. This involved a lot of taxi rides and eating out in fine restaurants. We tucked into fresh sardines along with fresh salad and lobsters, an old favourite that always transports me back to Dominica, where Papa Juslin specialised in lobster fishing. Even shopping was a pleasure. I bought Michelle CoCo Chanel perfume and other things that she requested. I bought myself a number of crocodile belts and would've bought shoes to match if they had them in stock.

On that day we were in Cala D'or, and after shopping, we headed straight for the beach, which I'd actually seen on TV some months ago. It was a thrill to watch Leah take to the sea like a duck to water whereas Nathan had to be assured that it was all good and we were there for him. At some point, sea, time and space stood still, as we savoured heaven.

But we descended into hell soon enough, on our return to the house that I wanted to call a home. It made no difference that I ate from the same pot as everyone else. I felt impending doom, as the gap between us widened. I'd ask Michelle for a talk but, as always, it was no can do!

The house was well stocked with Bollinger champagne, Remy Martin, other fine cognacs, wines and spirits. I stuck to my favourite champagne and cognac. I began to smoke crack at certain addresses in the area, including the house of an acquaintance from Nigeria, who had spent many years in Philadelphia USA. He walked with a limp in consequence of jumping out of a fifth-floor apartment in New York. Every bone was broken except those in his back. Even one eye had to be returned to its socket. In reality, that jump was no such thing, but the result of a coke deal that went wrong. As long as I had crack, I was welcome to knock on his door at any time.

One day, I called at his house to be greeted by his son with the news that his dad had passed away from a heroin overdose. In shock, I recalled the time I lifted his dad in a pub, threw him down on his back, and picked up a stool to smash over his head. I didn't follow through, as the manager intervened with an imploring look. That was when he'd called me a pussycat, after I had foot all the bills for drinking, eating and cabbing everywhere, with him in tow.

I slept with a number of ladies in different houses, close to home, as my marriage seemed to be in irreversible decline. Some I met at clubs, others in pubs. However, one lady I met was introduced to me by Tony, the Italian fraudster friend of mine. Her name was Jerry and she was telepathic. I felt at home with her and spent a fortnight, taking her out to dinner and parties, with constant drinking and snorting of cocaine.

Not only was Jerry telepathic, she never seemed to get drunk either. After a fortnight, I returned to the house, immediately packed the biggest suitcase with some of my clothes and returned to Jerry's. I had to make a short about turn though, because Jerry made it clear that she'd rather live alone. She said she'd rather not be in a sexual relationship, as she would lose her power of telepathy. She's the only person

I've ever met who constantly knew my thoughts and could respond to what I was thinking, instead of what I said. It was an amazing and unforgettable moment in my life.

I was secretive in moving out and in moving back in. Sometime later, I went to the pub Jerry and I frequented. At some point I argued with the barman, but for what? I don't remember. I also called a group of men wankers, and rejected the advances of a woman, who happened to be the wife of a villain. As I left the pub, I threw my glass of Guinness behind the bar.

Before my feet touched the pavement, I was twice hit on the back of the head with a baseball bat. As I hit the ground, someone tried to cut my throat, while others put the boot in. I was aware that there were at least six assailants, as I focused on the guy with the knife. By the grace of God, I managed to overpower the knifeman, and got to my feet. I was surprised that my adversaries fled, instead of continuing the fight.

Having developed a full-blown rage, I proceeded to a house where I knew they hung out and beat the living daylights out of Dodge. He wasn't one of the assailants, but in my rage, I decided that he'd have to take some blows on their behalf. This resulted in a vendetta. I had to be careful on the streets. On one occasion, a car came out of the parking lot with headlights on at full beam and accelerated towards me, as I began to cross the road. I stepped back just in time. The driver was the same guy who had tried to cut my throat.

The gang eventually sent an intermediary to discuss peace, but I wasn't interested. I told him that I still remembered the kicking I received and was in no mood for peace. My pride was still hurting.

Nevertheless, after several meetings at my house with the intermediary, we drew a line under our differences. I had my skull x-rayed and was given the all clear. I also had a chipped tooth fixed in the wake of all this mayhem. My recuperation, if you can call it that, was an increased intake of alcohol, crack and cocaine. The void within me darkened, deepened and widened, as the pain and loneliness grew. I was a popular man all over London, but completely alone.

Suddenly, I was reaching for the champagne, early in the morning, thinking that it was okay. I couldn't wait for the pubs to open in order to leave the house.

My dreams of writing beautiful songs in my marital home were shattered. In fact, every time I headed for the house, it was as if a dark cloud came along and blotted out the sunlight. I wanted us to live as a loving and peaceful family but that wasn't happening. The arrival of Nathan and Leah made no difference, and that hurt me deeply.

As Michelle could never find time for an honest chat, the guilt, shame, regret and resentment I felt grew even more painful. I felt that I was letting myself, and all my children down. I also felt that I was letting down my wider family and all those who respected me. In fact, I felt like I was plummeting into the bottomless pit of Mamie's prophecy.

Michelle called the police on me on several occasions, as my temper flared. On one occasion, it was about me coming in at eleven a.m. from a night-club. On another, I threatened to kill her with a flick knife in my hand, and once, I even threatened to burn the house down. In a grip of paranoia, rage and frustration, I once whipped her with a fencing sword during her pregnancy. Furthermore, I pursued her into the A & E and attacked her with a barrage of verbal abuse as the doctor examined her for any damage that those lashes may have caused. The only concern was for Michelle and the twins. As my drug and alcoholic rage, frustration and paranoia diminished, regret, remorse, guilt and shame took their place.

I couldn't accept my powerlessness over people, places and things, and desperately wanted to fix our marriage, for everyone's sake. I needed her co-operation and wasn't getting it. To be constantly criticised about his family, friends, clothes, eating habits and business affairs, would have tried the patience of a saint, which I definitely was not. Drinking and drugging didn't help either.

These arguments with Michelle resulted in me being remanded in custody for one month at first. A month later, I was imprisoned for another month, and then released on bail, to appear at Wood Green Crown Court. I was charged with possession and intent to supply two kilos of marijuana, that

Michelle had handed to the police. She had given them a load of bicarbonate of soda, thinking it was cocaine. I was acquitted, but endured police harassment because I called them liars in court.

They'd stop and search me as I left my front door, or even in the park at the back of the house, when I was with, or without the babies. My friends advised me to leave this loveless marriage, but I hung on for Nathan and Leah. I didn't want to fail them, as I had the others, by not being at home to bring them up.

Sleepless nights followed, and no amount of champagne and cognac could put me to asleep. As I fought to kick the coke and crack habit, it was replaced with five days and nights of heavy drinking without sleep. When I visited my doctor and complained about my insomnia, I was diagnosed as depressed and he prescribed antidepressants. I refused to accept his diagnosis and avoided taking the medication.

I believed that if Michelle and I got on, the stepchildren would get on with me too. I couldn't believe how I got myself into that situation in the first place. I told Michelle, that as soon as Nathan and Leah knew me one hundred percent as their dada, I'd leave. She laughed and said, "Go right ahead." This was during a fleeting conversation that we had in the kitchen.

In a bid to reconnect with the music business, I visited Steel Pulse. Their chef, Slue was my friend from borstal days. I visited them regularly, and with Michelle and the babies on one occasion. They were located at Jacobs, in Farnborough, a mansion equipped with two beautiful recording studios, living quarters, and an outdoor swimming pool.

Steel Pulse had a chemistry that turned into magic as they recorded their tracks. It was a privilege and a pleasure to support their creativity. I've never met a nicer group of musicians, and Slue's cooking was Michelin star quality. My friend had taken his experience from the borstal kitchen to another level.

My infidelity continued, as I took a beautiful young lady to a hotel after scoring some coke in West London. I no longer liked having sex without it and alcohol. I felt ashamed and resentful about being diagnosed with depression. My only answer was to self-medicate.

Then, I met Helen at a shebeen, in a house I used to run past as a schoolboy, in cross country races. She was a woman I'd fancied years before, and I was glad to get my hands on her. We'd rendezvous at different hotels, where we'd drink and drug and have sex for days and nights, with intervals in between. We got on so well that I wished she was my wife instead. Sadly, Helen didn't tell me that she couldn't have children, and there I was, busy trying to get her pregnant. It wouldn't have made any difference, as the chemistry between us, sexually, was on fire. We stopped meeting at hotels when I rented a property close to my marital address.

It was there that I burst into tears, as all the coke and alcohol failed to numb the pain. Helen asked me what was wrong. I said I missed my babies and could hear their innocent voices calling me. Returning to them sounded like a good idea, until I remembered the relentless hostility of my wife and stepchildren, especially the teenaged twins.

I discovered that you can't buy love, as all the money I threw at that marriage didn't make one bit of a difference. Eventually, I moved out into an apartment in docklands with Helen, and not one day or night went by without us drinking and coking. Once, Michelle found me in a pub with Helen and threw a pint of lager in my face. She also visited me in docklands and over a meal at a nearby restaurant in Tobacco Dock, I agreed, in Anthony's presence, to return to the house at her request.

Seven days later, I was met with a hostile reception from Simone. She got on the phone with her mother, who denied that we'd gotten back together. I left the house feeling embarrassed and returned to docklands without even seeing the babies. I felt that the stepchildren didn't want Nathan and Leah to have a dad around, as they never had their dad at home either.

In fact, on one occasion, before I left the house, I was sentenced to ten months imprisonment for possession of sensi weighing two pounds. While I was away, the teenage twins threatened to leave home if I returned to the house on my release. Consequently, when I turned my key in the front door on my return, it didn't open. I got into the house after ringing the bell, only to find that all my clothes were missing from my wardrobe and were packed at my sister Verina's place.

At Docklands, I felt angry with myself, walking Helen's dog around the green, because I thought I ought to be walking with my little twins instead. They'd just started primary school and I made sure I arrived at the house in time to accompany them on their first day. Michelle didn't go with us and I resented that, as I feared for the welfare of Nathan and Leah.

At three years old, was this the beginning of my criminal career.

Family photo with parents and siblings.
Back row from left to right: Vander Pierre, Rupert Pierre, Mama
Jean Pierre and Verina Pierre
Front row from left to right: Glen Pierre, Sandra Pierre and
Heather Pierre

Mama Jean with stepfather Clive Anderson, in their heyday.

Mama Jean, our beauty queen.

My spiritual mother Mamie, otherwise known as Lady Ina Valerie.

My youngest sister Antigua Jade on a visit at Elvis Presley's place.

Chapter 14

Paranoia, Psychosis and Beyond

Back at Docklands, I managed to get arrested on my way back to the apartment, after buying a bottle of cognac around ten a.m., to help me come down from the coke. I drank half the bottle before I returned to the block and ended up at the police station instead. I shouted abuse at the police and the doctor who came to see me and was transferred to the psychiatric unit at the Royal London Hospital in Whitechapel.

I refused to stay there, and the police were called to escort me back to the police station, where I was charged for having counterfeit traveller cheques in my possession. The charge was thrown out of court, at my very first appearance. About this time, my relationship with Helen began to feel strained. I realised that she was someone to have a good time with, but not to live with. The pain of my descent into darkness continued.

It was during that phase that I met Jane from Holland Park. She drank copious amounts of wine with me and after some weeks, she invited me to live with her. She was educated, with a middle-class background, but had anger management and control issues. I agreed to live with her, as I thought I was able to run more than one home at a time.

She became very upset when I mentioned that my twins would have to stay with us from time to time. For her that was a no-no. She then left to get a set of keys cut for me. The thought of my children being unable to stay with me while I was at Jane's ended in my leaving the house before she returned with my set of keys.

Jane became aware of Helen and Helen became aware of Jane, via telephone conversations that were meant to be private. Jane had been listening in on the other line. In the midst of all that, I'd also spent some time at my sister's place. That was after all my clothes had been transferred there while I was in prison. Verina was very supportive, although she had difficulties of her own, coming to terms with being abandoned by her husband, six months into a marriage and six months pregnant.

This was in a house she had just bought after getting married. Ken, her husband, never moved in there with her. Verina bought him a brand-new car and financed the purchase of his flat, which he let out after abandoning her and the baby, to go to live with a woman in New York.

I tried to reciprocate her support, but it wasn't easy, because coke, crack and alcohol had clearly taken over my life. I'd be smoking crack and drinking alcohol in that shoe box room she let me occupy, feeling angry and sorry for myself at nights, while she slept with her baby James, two rooms away.

I erupted into anger one night, as I looked at the direction my life was taking. Verina got scared and ran out of the house, with baby James in her arms. She ended up at our sister Hetty's place. That incident sobered me up, as I sat in her house, feeling like some kind of monster, lost and unloved for all eternity.

I kept asking myself, why is my life like this? Why? I agonised over the answer. I didn't hear it. I was too drunk and drugged to hear it. I didn't reveal any of my difficulties to my friends, as I feared they'd laugh at me. "The doctor diagnosed me as depressed!" "I'm in pain!" "I'm afraid to go home!" These exclamations weren't in the gangster's dialogue. These were signs of weakness. They didn't project the right image. Honest dialogue is part of the healing process, but I chose to suffer in silence. I chose to remain as sick as my secrets.

I suffered in silence, laughing and joking through the pain, protecting my bruised and battered ego with a wall of denial, defiance and dishonesty.

In the midst of this fragmented existence, I also stayed in the house of Roy, a solicitor friend of mine. His wife had left him, and we became a support system for each other, as we went through the experiences of being estranged from our wives. In my case, from my children as well. We played chess, but my mind was elsewhere. Helen spent time with me at his house and when his wife returned, I moved out and rented a flat in Tottenham. An arrangement that was very short-lived, as I was visited by the police, looking for ganja. As I left the flat with the police and a bag of ganja, which they'd found in the loft, I was told by the landlord: "Don't come back, unless it's to pick up your belongings!" I felt like I was living in a world of rejection but stopped short of recognising that my choices and actions were orchestrating everything.

After that incident with the police in the docklands, which included being under surveillance from a commercial building across the road as well as on the streets, Helen moved out and I went to live at Mamie's. We continued to see each other for a while, as our relationship fizzled out.

At Mamie's, I spoke to Michelle on the phone, about us seeing a marriage counsellor, only to discover that her ex, Glen, had moved back in. Marriage counselling was no longer an option. Mamie was distressed to see me in so much pain and alarmed at my consumption of alcohol. She advised me to drink less. She had no idea of my coke habit at the time.

I became friends with a brother, Tony, who passed away during a drunken brawl when he hit the pavement on the Stonebridge Estate in Harlesden. I wasn't present at the time. I filled the gap when I befriended some schoolteachers and assorted professionals, to get some normality in my life. We visited each other's homes for dinner parties, with a lot of boozing in the process. They were lovely people, but I lost touch with them when Mamie moved into sheltered housing after a stroke.

I was riddled with guilt, remorse and regret, as I thought my behaviour was instrumental in causing that. Mamie's home was too small for a dinner party, so we held it at Percy's place when it was my turn. He had an honours degree in zoology, and was an ex-postman, seeking a new job at the time. I rented a room in a house in Wandsworth soon after Mamie's move. It was there that I got another girlfriend, Faye. I eventually moved in with her in West Hampstead, although I still kept my room in Bassingham Road. She had a lovely daughter, Naiomi, and we got on well. I continued to see my children as often as I could, but often let them down because I decided to have a drink first.

Drink and drugs always led me away from my responsibilities, and fuelled a cycle of more guilt, shame, regret and remorse. I was on my way to Faye's one day, stopping at every alcoholic watering hole en-route. Day turned to night as I entered a club by the Finchley Road. I got into an argument, while in a blackout, with a group of men and sobered up after receiving a karate kick to the back of my left knee. I exited the club, masking the intense pain from the blow to the knee that kept me awake all night thereafter.

After visits to hospitals, north and south of the river, I eventually discovered I had a torn ligament and cartilage. It wasn't operated on, as the surgeon said it appeared to be healing by itself. I was on crutches for about eighteen months. I found myself abstaining from crack at that time but drank heavily instead. I now understand that my behaviour was something called cross addiction.

Still limping, I wrote poems, and frequented the local off-licence, and a wine bar called LJs. Without coke and crack in the equation, I eventually joined LJ's cricket team. We played matches on Wandsworth Common with boxes of Molson lager on ice, and lovely Australian ladies to cheer us on. It felt good to have some normality in my life, interacting with others, instead of the crack pipe in secret.

However, deep down, I knew I had a problem, as drinking alcohol in the morning became routine, as I strove to resist crack and cocaine. The battle made me feel ill-at-ease, sandwiched between alcoholism and crack addiction. I couldn't visualise life without any drugs at all. Marijuana didn't come into the equation, although it had been my one and only habit before the war started.

As the grip of alcoholism tightened on me, I visited Mr Russo, my doctor, revealed my concerns, and asked for an implant, to help me stop drinking. I was given a blood test and was told that my liver and everything else was in good shape and not to worry. Furthermore, my revelations of crack and cocaine abuse prompted my doctor to ask me if I could get him some cocaine. Surprised by his request, I said I could, but didn't follow it through.

Jane phoned me one day and suggested that I get enrolled into a hotel and catering course, as I was a good cook with a lot of time, doing nothing but drink alcohol. I joined the course just to fill my time and passed it with distinction. The lecturer offered me work as a Food Technician, which meant being his assistant. He assured me of a job placement as a manager in a top London restaurant, after I gained more experience under his management.

I found myself storing cans of Tennent's super strong lager in my locker and slipping into the changing room every so often for a drink. I hated Tennent's! It reminded me of homeless alcoholics, drinking on park benches and in shop doorways. I swore I'd never drink that. I hated the taste and the smell, but then again, I liked the effect of the cheap alcohol. I drank it, feeling less of a person than I was before, even when it sat in a brown paper bag.

My heart said I was going to end up homeless and financially ruined just like those Tennent's drinkers I feared becoming. My head, on the other hand, said I'd never be broke, nor homeless, nor begging or committing petty crimes, in order to buy alcohol, crack and cocaine. I failed to realise that I was already on that road, as I gulped down the cheap strong lager.

My wage at the college wasn't enough to live on, as it just about covered the rent. As a result, I spent a month's pay over the weekend, as the crack habit returned. I snorted coke in the college toilet, and became so paranoid, I thought our boss, Brian, knew what I was up to. It was a stressful situation, and the more I took coke to relieve the stress, I ended up reliving it instead, terrified that my dark destructive habits would come to light.

Brian put me out of my misery by sacking me one Saturday, after he caught me sleeping in my hideout. I'd just been paid and hadn't slept the night before. Although the sack hurt my pride, I was glad to be free to drink and drug as I pleased. I no longer had to chew garlic to disguise the smell of alcohol as I strolled around the Hammersmith and West London College.

I had grown resentful towards Brian, as the wages I received were more suited to someone living at home with their parents. I only took the job believing that it was a step up the ladder to a better position within six months. That dream job didn't materialise, and gave me a feeling of being used, as he left me on occasions to do his job as well as mine, for a pittance. I was impatient, as my mind raced into the past and the future but was hardly ever in the present moment. Being in the present moment meant I had to have instant gratification through drugs, alcohol and sex. I was unable to accept life on life's terms.

I remembered tears falling from my eyes, as I watched television at Mamie's and wondered what was happening to me. I remembered going out for walks at three and four a.m., climbing over park fences and tearfully hugging trees, crying to God to help me. I felt there was no one that I could talk to, who would understand what I was going through. I was wandering through a dark tunnel with no light in sight. I wondered if anyone could see the pain in my face or hear it in my laughter. There seemed to be no end to this.

My ego refused to be deflated, and I used fine clothes and the money in my pocket to fool the public. I was the house that looked good on the outside but was crumbling and bare on the inside.

Suicidal thoughts came forcefully to me, suggesting I leap under incoming trains. In such moments, I held my back against the wall, well away from the platform edge, terrified at the thought of anyone observing the fear that tormented me. On other occasions, I had to avoid walking across bridges as compelling thoughts of jumping into the Thames constantly came from nowhere. I also had to abandon driving completely, as these forceful thoughts urged me to drive through the barrier on the flyover, or crash into cars, instead of driving the Mercedes safely to my good friend Jimmy's home. He was a highly intelligent and dangerous gangster with a very spiritual side, and I was best man at his wedding. After successfully following his lead home, I never revealed those suicidal thoughts to him, although we were really close, and I knew that he had mental health issues of his own. I thank God in my heart as I safely parked the car at his doorstep.

It was frightening, and I knew it wasn't me. These weren't my thoughts. So where were they coming from? It was frightening!

The spirituality Mamie introduced me to as a child, helped me through such moments, and gave me strength when I was weak. There was no way that I was going to associate with gangsters in that shape. I could imagine their reactions if they heard me say that my doctor had diagnosed me as depressed or that something was telling me to jump in front a train. That kind of conversation was taboo in my circles. As a result, I became reclusive, elusive and isolated.

By that time, I'd moved from Bassingham Road in Earlsfield, near Wandsworth prison, to Putney, and spent a lot of time with Mamie at her new address at 13 Alexander Court, Queensbury. I drank, smoked crack and snorted cocaine abusively there. This involved spending hours in her bathroom. She'd knock on the door full of concern, asking me what was I doing in there. After I told her the truth, she invited me to smoke openly in her front room instead of hiding.

"Is she joking?" I thought. "Has she smoked crack?" I smoked one pipe in Mamie's presence and felt like garbage, full of regret, remorse, guilt and shame. My heart and soul cried out in pain, as the void within grew bigger and darker. I didn't think Mamie would like me to close her curtains on a sunny day, so I used to get anxious and impatient for her to retire to bed, leaving me free to smoke crack. She continued to tell me to cut down on my drinking and surprised me by having a drop of lager in the tiniest shot glass.

I loved Mamie, and I knew I was hurting her. I knew I was hurting my children too, by frequently failing to appear as planned. I knew I was hurting my family and friends. I knew

I was hurting myself. All these reasons, together with many drink and drug related imprisonments, couldn't stop me from alcohol, coke and crack abuse. I felt people were stupid not to get high on something in this terrible world.

I didn't approve of heroin or other manufactured drugs, so that put me on a pedestal. I didn't want to stop taking drugs. I simply wanted to drink and drug like a gentleman. Have one or two lines of coke for the night, a glass or two of champagne and cognac, and one spliff for the day. Walk away from an unfinished glass or bottle of alcohol. One blast of the crack-pipe for the day and leave it at that. I wanted to be like one of those who could do that sort of thing naturally, without ever getting hooked. I battled to keep my addiction under control. At the time, I wasn't aware that some people have a mental and physical allergy or attraction to alcohol and drugs that leads them into addiction, and I was one of them.

Oblivious to all this, I carried on writing songs and poems as well as a novel. I was still seeing Jane and another lady intermittently but spent more time with Faye. There was a woman I had a relationship with on Faye's doorstep. Faye blew up into a fireball as soon as she found out. She threatened me, saying that she'd get a close friend of the family to shoot me, and claimed that she owned a gun herself.

She toured the pubs from northwest to West London, looking for me. She found me in the Slug and Lettuce at Notting Hill, with a lovely lady called Philomena. Faye threatened her like a gangster, causing her to flee instantly. I was high on coke and booze and looking forward to bedding Philly. My plan had been thwarted and I was upset, but kept my cool, as Faye raged on. I went onto the kerb, to see in which direction Philomena had gone but she'd disappeared. Faye spoke to me with such venom that the management called the police. I walked away into the night, towards a music producer's house in the area. His name was Mark and it was there that I met Gil Scott-Heron. He sat in a chair, crack pipe in hand, in a world of his own.

I got some coke, then went on to a shebeen in Ladbroke Grove, where I befriended two lovely ladies who introduced me to a cool club on Green Street, Green Park, sometime after five in the morning. I stayed there with them till about nine a.m., making regular trips to the loo to hoover white lines. Everyone was in vogue to the music of soul and RnB.

My flat in Putney remained unfurnished for years, as drinking and drugging became my priority. Things I said I'd never do returned to haunt me.

Like picking up dog ends from the pavement, in a bid to keep all the money in my pocket for crack and alcohol. I did it when I thought no one was looking. I'd break up the dog ends in a pouch and pretend it was rolling tobacco. I was filled with shame, bewilderment and disbelief at how low I'd sunk. I became a witness to my descent in the bottomless pit. But a big drink up, and some big hits on the crack pipe would fumigate and wash away the torture of existing in the present moment.

I arrived at the point where I hated waking up and looked forward to the oblivion of sleep. So, whenever I awoke, I immediately sought sleep by reaching for the bottle or can of whatever, to escort me there. I couldn't face the public without alcohol in my system. The thought of running out of coke, crack and alcohol scared me. Sometimes, I found myself lying to my mum and stepfather. For example, I'd say there were Yardies waiting for me in my flat and I needed money to get rid of them or it could get nasty.

I became a serial shoplifter in order to feed my habit, as my finances and business connections disappeared. I didn't have the strength to hold on to them. I'd ask strangers in the streets to help me out with my cab fare home. I think being well-dressed helped my cause. I committed fraud and would pick up any purse or wallet or other valuables that were unattended.

Mamie's prophecy was being fulfilled. The pain was getting worse as I fell further into the bottomless pit, which at other times, felt like a dark tunnel, without a pinhead of light to be seen. When the pain got too much, I'd go out into the woods on Putney Heath and scream before first light, with no one around. Those birds and foxes must have wondered what the hell was going on. I began to wish I was one of them, so I wouldn't have any need for drugs and alcohol.

I furnished the flat after five years, with Faye's help. On one occasion, while she was in the sitting room sipping red wine, I pretended I needed more ingredients for the meal I was preparing, as a sudden and overwhelming craving for crack came over me. In a euphoric recall, I'd get high and excited, just thinking of the glass bottle, filling with creamy cloudy smoke, that got thicker and creamier, until it appeared like a bottle of milk, with a burning gauze as a cork. Those fancy crack pipes had long gone, as I was using Martel miniature bottles instead. When in possession of cocaine, I was a powerful king who manipulated and controlled others, and without it, I was weak as a mouse.

At that time, I frequented a friend's house in Wembley. Prem was famous for sleeping with royalty, and notorious for attempting to strangle a policeman whilst in handcuffs. At his place, I saw how a family home gradually became a crack house. We'd be in the backroom for days and nights smoking crack, chasing it with bottles of cognac, champagne, vodka and even Tennent's Super. That was the forbidden room from which his children and their mother were barred. It was an open house, and all were welcome, especially the man or woman delivering crack, the one who had it in their possession or the money to buy it.

I was amazed at how religiously he managed to cook for his children and visit the bookies on a daily basis. Once I hit that crack pipe, I wasn't moving, unless I had to go and get more. There were times when I'd leave the backroom, and investigate the house in a paranoid state, as I feared armed police and MI5 agents were at the windows, about to storm the building. I'd see shapes and shadows to convince me, especially at night. So many hours of paranoia turned into sweat. A sober person would say that it was their imagination, as they would've raided the house by now. But I kept holding on to the paranoia instead of letting it go. To let it go, I had to let go of the drinking and drugging.

Chapter 15

Crack House Hotel

Guilt, shame, regret and remorse, came up again and again, as I thought of Prem's children in the house. I was glad that they weren't mine. But those feelings receded with every gulp of alcohol and crack smoke, only to resurface later.

Once, I ventured into his garden, and left my crack on the ground while I investigated the bullshit going on in my head. When I returned to pick up my goods, they had disappeared from the face of the earth. Not short of money, I said nothing, and ordered another crack delivery. I looked at the other men's faces in the house and knew who'd taken it. In fact, I ended up buying my own crack twice--over. Incidents like that fuelled my hate and paranoia. Prem called crack and alcohol his daily medication. I witnessed the gulf that developed between him, his children and their mother, Annette. The gulf grew wider and wider, until she moved out with the children. That process took about three years, but it had started long before I visited the house as a crack smoker.

After they moved out, the place became a crack house, with crackheads, myself included, occupying every room. To leave my crack on the table, go to the loo, and expect to find the same size on my return, was being naively optimistic. I'd be lucky to find anything at all. Somehow, I didn't do that sort of thing, and if I smoked someone else's crack, I'd say so. I also refused to trade crack for a shine from a woman. I gave it to them unconditionally.

I had to threaten others, slap a gunman in the face, and reach for my knife, as people tried to steal my crack, pick money from my pocket, or show me disrespect, as I romanced with the crack pipe.

I remember finding half a twenty-pound note on a fat wad of twenties, still held in place with the elastic band. I pretended to be oblivious to all that dirty behaviour, while I raged inside. I wanted to kill others, while I was slowly committing suicide myself.

Fed up with the dog-eat-dog mentality, I became a recluse in my flat on Putney Hill. I longed for the days when we smoked like gentlemen around the table, but those days were long gone! I visited the Greenman Pub by Putney Heath, where Dick Turpin used to drink. There, I made several trips to the outside toilets in order to warm up my crack pipe, as I fantasised about a long-haired leggy blonde at the bar. I should've approached her instead of fantasising about it. By the time I was ready to talk to her, she had vacated the building.

I ate a lot of garlic and raw lemons and drank a lot of herbal concoctions from the health food shop, in a bid to detoxify and keep some sort of balance. I knew I was poisoning my body, but I always intended to quit tomorrow, after one last big drink and drug up. Tomorrow never came! The trees on Putney Heath became my best friends. I was baffled, as I saw no end to this ritual of living to use and using to live.

In isolation, I was visited by various crack dealers, and found neighbouring places where I could score. My life was dictated by addiction. There were times when I was desperate to come down from crack and cocaine, choosing to wait for the grocer off-licence to open at six thirty in the morning, riven with anxiety. I'd be outside the shop long before it opened. I was a slave to alcohol and drugs.

Although it was unlawful to sell alcohol so early in the morning, I'd help myself and leave the money on the counter. Sometimes, I simply helped myself. That habit got worse, as I found myself wheeling trolleys out of supermarkets, laden to the brim with bottles of their best champagne and cognac.

On one occasion, but without a trolley, I found myself dashing out of Waitrose supermarket with two large bottles of whiskey, and a security guard in pursuit. I dashed across Putney High Street, without looking right or left into busy traffic from both directions. I'd risked my life for a drink! Oblivious to that fact at the time, I was just glad to get away and get that whiskey down me as fast as I could, while I mourned the loss of the other bottle that I had dropped on the pavement.

I entered a phase where I'd be going somewhere, only to find myself waking up in a police cell instead. They offered me help, but I refused it, as I wouldn't admit that I was addicted to anything, and that included alcohol. My pride and self-delusion refused to accept the truth.

I wouldn't acknowledge my destructive relationships, believing that the few good moments outweighed the million bad ones. So, there I was one day, at Helen's place near Blackfriars Bridge, drinking and smoking crack, in between sexual activities. I suddenly felt a dark cloud come over me. I decided to leave, taking my bag of coke with me as she couldn't be trusted.

I hid the coke under someone's hedge, as I began to feel terribly ill. My shoes and clothes were suffocating me. My body needed to breathe, as I walked along the Embankment at five o'clock in the morning, peeling off my dark pinstripe suit until, finally, I was down to my boxer shorts. Suicidal impulses gripped me, almost as if the River Thames was inviting me to jump in and end my suffering. But I kept on walking. People in passing cars noticed me. I didn't care. I was in a lot of agony, and so grateful, when the police took me to a psychiatric unit. By the time I saw the psychiatrist, I'd come down from the coke, crack and alcohol, or perhaps I ought to say, I'd ascended from the pit of despair. Anyway, the psychiatrist declared that I was sane.

As finances grew tighter, I stole my Mamie's pension book on several occasions, knowing that she lived from hand to mouth and wouldn't have any money for her weekly shopping. Furthermore, I stole the money she saved to go to visit her brother, my great uncle Austin, in New Rochelle, New York. I justified it by telling myself that I'd soon pay her back, but never did.

I suffered so much guilt, shame, regret and remorse, that the drugs and alcohol didn't work. All that pain was reinforced when I stole some CDs from my stepfather, after he and my mum refused to give me any more money, no matter how chilling the tale. After drinking and smoking crack from the sale of the CDs, I was outside their house, two or three hours later, to ask for their forgiveness, as I was overwhelmed with guilt and shame. My stepfather simply responded by saying I'd better hop it, or else he'd call the police. I left feeling like a dog, with his tail between his legs. I wouldn't be returning to that house anytime soon.

I felt so raw and sensitive, that nearly everything became painful. My enthusiasm for life had disappeared. My thirst for money had left me a long time ago, and only resurfaced when I needed to get more crack, cocaine and alcohol. Losing the hunger and drive to accumulate money, baffled me. I figured that I could always raise more cash, once I'd cleaned up for a few months. That became an impossibility when I realised my inability to abstain from drink and drugs, even for one hour, never mind a day. I settled for petty crime instead; the addict in me couldn't wait. I was so weak, unable to do the deal that would bring in the big bucks to feed my habit.

Cooking, cleaning and shopping became a chore, instead of a pleasure. Personal hygiene fell from bathing twice a day, to whenever I could fit it in between the bottle and the crack pipe. I was in agony, as my soul cried out from deep within.

I began to wonder whether clinical depression might be the root of all my problems. After seeing three doctors, I settled for Doctor North. She expressed care and compassion. She was a doctor, not just by title, but by vocation. She alerted me to the fact that alcohol is a depressant, and that antidepressants are useless to a drinker. It made sense, but I refused to stop drinking. I was a slave to substance abuse. I was afraid to reveal my crack and coke habit to her, because I couldn't bear to be seen as a drug addict. I remained ignorant of the fact that alcohol is a drug.

Asking for help was a sticking point for me, but I managed to ask her after much deliberation. With Doctor North's help, I was offered a place at Mount Carmel, a rehab unit in

Streatham. On the day I was to be admitted, I had no money and couldn't find my travel pass. I phoned the rehab to notify them of the situation and was frustrated by having to leave a message on the answer machine. In effect, I had sabotaged my own treatment, with the rampant disease of drug addiction.

Crack and cocaine may be white, but it carried a dark and negative energy that turned my face ashen grey. No amount of soap and water could wash it away. Only abstinence restored my complexion. Being cross-addicted, total abstinence was out of the question. It didn't seem possible and that thought never occurred to me. Living like a recluse, I continued to write songs, poems and a novel in my flat. I became acquainted with crackheads, Yardies, and other drug dealers on the Winstanley Estate at Clapham Junction. I would score on the estate and immediately return to Putney and the crack pipe.

That suddenly changed when I found myself visiting crack houses on the estate, instead of scoring on a staircase in a block of flats, and then heading back to Putney. I had sworn I'd never visit or frequent crack houses, and that further fall from grace haunted me.

People, some with mental health issues, were allowing Yardies to turn their flats into crack dens. Some of them became homeless as a result. I always turned down offers to use my flat. I would have no privacy if I let it to Yardies. I needed to be on my own. I didn't want the chaos that came with it either, including confrontation for control of my flat. Payment of one sixteenth or more of crack per day to use my flat, didn't appeal to me at all, although I was an addict.

I was glad when I found a gangster on the estate who'd deliver to my place in Putney. It didn't feel like a home, even with furniture. It was just an apartment, somewhere to smoke crack and drink alcohol anyway I pleased, without having to worry about my crack disappearing while I used the bathroom.

Faye, from West Hampstead, paid me a visit one day. I decided to cook us a meal. Suddenly, an overwhelming craving for crack had me making excuses about needing more ingredients for the meal. I went out and scored more crack instead. I pretended the shop didn't have what I was looking for. While Faye sipped red wine in the sitting room, I left things simmering on the stove while I slipped into the bathroom to heat the crack pipe. I eventually emerged from the bathroom to find the front door wide open. Faye had made her exit, without a word or a sound. I never saw her again.

More thoughts and emotions of guilt, shame, regret and remorse arose, as I recalled Faye and I driving to the bank to get some money to support my habit, but she didn't know that. Along the way, whilst driving through Fulham, she received a phone-call that informed her of her father's passing. Instead of consoling her, I asked her to get a move on before the bank closed. I was horrified at what I'd become but felt powerless to change it.

Faye's father, Gus, was a big man of Jewish extraction, and always smartly dressed in a shirt and tie. He was a friend of the Kray Twins and an ex-club owner in London's West End. I had the pleasure of meeting him on my own for a drink at a pub in St John's Wood, and at a family union at his youngest daughter's home in Barnes, during the festive season, with Faye. Little did I know then that that incident with Faye, along with many others, would one day prompt me, to write 'The Walk of Shame.'

In the silence of my room, I eagerly awaited sleep, after another round of drink and drugs. I surfaced hours later, or so it seemed, to the sound of Shola's voice, the one who passed away from a heroin overdose. My eyes remained closed, and my body motionless, in impenetrable darkness. Visually, I saw nothing. Our communication was telepathic. Without moving my lips, I asked him what was it like to be dead. He gave no response. I repeated the same question to no avail. Then I changed my question to, "Why did you do it?" He said the heroin was too strong and had sent him to the grave.

He returned several months later to tell me that his current condition was worse than his worst situation on earth. I asked him if it was like that for everyone. He said no, and that there were different levels. His last words were, "I'm waiting to see His Majesty!" For me, that was proof that there was another life after life on earth. Later, I wondered what I would tell my creator when I got to the other side, "Sorry, but all I did was drink and do drugs." I became increasingly haunted and horrified by the thought.

Deep down, my resolve to change my ways had been strengthened, although nothing on the surface had changed. I was arrested seventeen times for shoplifting during my last four years as a user. I frequented the crack houses more and more, as I couldn't wait to get home once I'd scored. Once I started smoking in that chaos, I'd be there for days. As I sat in the desert of insanity and active addiction of the crack house, I declared from time to time how I was going to kick the habit one day and return to the music business. My words fell on deaf ears.

I'd sing and dance through my pain in the crack house. During such moments, the Yardies would talk about taking me to Jamaica to do some shows. It didn't matter whether they meant it or not. I knew that they were confirming my talent as a singer-songwriter. They'd brighten up and ask me for a song when I entered the crack house and occasionally gave me crack for free, in appreciation for my singing and dancing.

You'd find me in the crack house in a Saville Row suit and crocodile shoes. Sometimes, I changed and bathed three times a day, in my efforts to stay fresh, and fool the public into thinking that I was okay. A bottle of aftershave lasted no more than seven days as I splashed and sprayed on more than I needed, in order to disguise the stench of alcohol seeping from my pores. I'd spray or splash my clothes as well as my body and mainly wore suits, smart casuals, expensive shoes and coats. I appeared a natty dresser on the outside but felt like a weak and empty fool on the inside. I felt like a tightened coil, a time bomb waiting to explode from within.

As money became scarcer, and doors shut in my face, I found myself being charged for shoplifting. I was banned from all Tesco and Sainsbury supermarkets in London. I'm grateful to the security guards who asked me why I was stooping so low, when they could see a better man than that in me.

The resulting seventeen arrests included many short prison sentences. On one occasion, I returned to Wandsworth prison within twenty-four hours of my release and was reallocated to the same cleaning job and the same cell, on the same wing. I feared becoming institutionalised, as I found these prison sentences a welcome break from the stress, strain and abuse afflicting my mind, body and spirit. I worried about the fact that I'd stopped praying every day on the outside but found it easy to do so in jail.

Every time I left prison and swore I'd never return to the crack house, I always made a b-line to the off-licence, to buy a celebratory bottle of champagne. There were also occasions when I couldn't wait to get out to warm the crack pipe. I'd rehearse in my cell with an imaginary crack pipe, to see for how long I could suck in air. The bigger the rock on the pipe, the longer I'd have to suck in air, and the bigger the buzz would be. Therefore, I was rehearsing for the real thing. In fact, my life was centred around drugs and alcohol, and escape from reality.

Halfway through my string of seventeen arrests, a social worker warned me that I was heading for homelessness, if I continued along the same path. The truth in her statement scared me! My habit, however, continued. Crack smoking had reached epidemic proportions, as I noticed more and more people were being imprisoned for drink and drug related offences.

Chapter 16

A House is Not a Home

One day, as I entered my flat, I was greeted by the buzzing sound of a blanket of flies on my sitting room wall. I lashed them all away with a kitchen towel, and went to bed, exhausted from drinking and drugging, with the intention of clearing up the flies from the floor as soon as I awoke. I awoke to find not one single fly on the carpet.

There were times when I looked in the kitchen and rifled amongst the wall rack of clothing in my bedroom, convinced that police or some nasty persons were hiding there, waiting to get at me. I'd see someone through the spy hole, but when I actually opened the front door, no one was there.

Suddenly, another "I will never be" was fulfilled, just as the social worker had predicted. I was summarily evicted from the flat that I'd hoped to buy and turn into a home one day. I had over seventy suits and pairs of shoes, about thirty overcoats, fine furniture and artworks on the walls, and simply left them all behind. All I took was a bag containing my songs, poems, and the novel I'd started. I deposited that bag at Prem's house for safe keeping. Is anything safe in a crack house?

I didn't report to the homeless people's unit, as directed. The off-licence was my first stop. That was my reaction to the crisis. My reaction was the same no matter what. As midnight approached, I remembered I had no keys to any of the millions of doors in this great big city. I couldn't believe it! It was either the park bench, or the crack den in the tower block at the Arndale Centre in Wandsworth. The crack house won.

After about five days, Mojo, the proprietor of the flat, asked me if I didn't have a home to go to, I told him that I was head of security and if anyone misbehaved, I would throw them out. I couldn't admit that I was homeless to anyone. Guilt, remorse and resentment, were killing me.

Instead of being a visitor, I was actually existing, and not living in a crack house. It was unreal, sleeping and waking up amidst all the chaos. Any valuables, including money and crack, had to be concealed inside my underwear before I went to sleep. No one had any morals or principles. There was a constant stream of stolen goods, all in the name of crack. The bathroom was so filthy that I preferred to urinate in the pub, or the park opposite.

In that hellhole, I became acquainted with many intelligent and talented people from good working- and middle-class backgrounds but that didn't make me feel any better about myself. After a fortnight without a bath, I got mad, descended to the shopping centre below, where I bought some bleach and Dettol disinfectant. Then I proceeded to clean the bath and toilet. I poured Dettol into the warm water, then sunk into the bath, ducking my head under the surface, and followed through with a good scrub. I left the bathroom with my body clean on the outside, but still feeling dirty inside.

I still hated waking up! I became tired of shoplifting and fraudulent practices. The merciless king, alcohol and the snow-queen insisted that I keep feeding my demons, those defects of character, that insanity.

My life wasn't just cracked, now it was completely fragmented, chaotic and confused. What had been arguably a pleasure, had become hard labour. I prayed to God to help me get away with what I was about to steal, and when I got caught, I'd ask him why.

On occasions, the magistrates said that they were willing to send me to rehab instead of prison, as it was clear that I needed help. All I had to do was admit in court that I was an alcoholic drug addict. After seeking help from Dr North, you'd think I'd jump at the chance.

However, I found myself unable to admit my addiction in a court of law, in front of a public gallery, because I wouldn't be able to walk the streets without fingers pointing at me. Or so I thought. I also thought that any admission of my inability to deal with drug and alcohol addiction would mean relinquishing what little power, control or pride, I had left.

I didn't understand at the time that admitting my powerlessness over drugs and alcohol actually empowered and earned me people's respect, through the power of honesty. It was the only way I could rebuild my self-respect, but my thinking was upside down. I believed the opposite. I was insane and didn't know it.

That crack house was frequented by murderers, killers, rapists, men of violence, liars, fraudsters, informers, prostitutes, pimps, burglars, pickpockets, thieves, robbers, conmen, lesbians, homosexuals, heterosexuals, bisexuals, bus drivers, labourers, civil servants, bankers, businessmen, singers, songwriters, musicians, the occasional pregnant woman, woman and her child, workers and professionals across the broad spectrum of society. It was society in miniature, on the dark side of life. Even in my anaesthetised state, I was humbled and ill at ease seeing pregnant women or a woman with her child in a crack house. Oddly enough, seeing teenagers in a crack house was something that didn't cause me concern. Now, in retrospect, I know I ought to have told them to go home. I should have told the pregnant women, and women with children to go home as well.

There are no morals in a crack house. It's the Broadway to Hell, or hell's waiting room on earth. I'm grateful to be free from that insanity, depravity and abominable existence, by the grace of God. My night out from the crack house was to go to the West End with some highly skilled and dangerous pickpockets, trawling the clubs and smoking crack in post-office red phone boxes, pretending to be on the phone. I actually heard a voice at the other end of the line without calling anyone. I kept things like that to myself. I didn't want anyone to think that I was insane. What I didn't know then was that I was as sick as my secrets. It really is good to talk to someone.

One day, I set about smashing furniture in the crack house as I came to believe that someone had stolen the crack out of my pocket, while I was using the pipe. Everybody vacated the flat as my temper flared. Only the dealers stayed. I turned my attention to them, by using a chair as a weapon. Calm was resumed after they phoned their Yardie boss, who told them to give me something to smoke, and pleaded with me to behave myself. The boss and I got on well.

I also got on with a shotter, the son of a great reggae artist, who also happened to be a victim of crack addiction. Every time a man and a woman went to the bathroom together, you knew sexual activity was taking place. I was in so much pain that alcohol, crack and cocaine made little difference, no matter how much I took. However, that didn't stop me from blocking the Yardies from entering the kitchen while my friend and I relieved someone of their crack. Another occasion saw me pushed out of the crack house in a drunken stupor, causing me to hit the ground outside the lift. I returned later, and almost ended up in a knife fight with the Yardie who had pushed me over earlier.

I was a tormented soul. Drained and stressed, I descended in the lift outside the crack house. I prayed to God for help. I had too much pride to go the homeless person's unit and ask for help, although I was beaten, battered and demolished.

I kept clinging to the idea of coming into some money that would enable me to get away from the mad, 'cockroached' environment that I was in at the time. I was arrested as I was about to re-enter the block with stolen goods, eager and anxious to engage with the crack pipe. That pipe became a person. It used to talk to me from near or far, even from the cupboard in the other room.

Chapter 17

Fellowship's First Stirrings

I asked God why had he allowed me to get arrested again? How could my arrest be of any help to me, as I heard the crack pipe calling me from the seventeenth floor? That was the beginning of my recovery, but I didn't know it at the time. People saw me as the gangster who fell from grace, but I didn't consider myself a gangster.

At the police station, I was seen by the doctor, who gave me Valium for the rough gloomy descent from alcohol, crack and cocaine. I noticed that I'd become keen on those awful microwave meals that they issued at the police station. Having not eaten for a few days, with the sudden absence of crack and alcohol, I was actually enjoying food that neither smelt nor tasted appetising before.

The police introduced me to a drug and alcohol worker and said that they'd ask the prosecution to recommend rehab to the court hearing my case. I saw and felt a compassionate side of the police that I'd never experienced before my descent into alcoholism and the crack-pit.

There was no loyalty or true friendship in the crack house. Again, in my humiliation, denial and pain, my pride and fear would not let me admit that I was a drug addict, but I was willing to concede that I was an alcoholic. It seemed more socially acceptable, as alcohol was something that was legally sold in the shops. However, in order to receive the support of the court, and the drug and alcohol services, I had to admit that I was a drug addict. I refused! I thought I'd lose any self-respect I had left. I was still unaware that the only way my self-respect would return was with honesty, and that alcohol is also a drug.

During my seven months imprisonment for shoplifting, I was allocated to the detox unit from the reception at Wandsworth prison. All my calls to my sister Verina went unanswered. All my letters to others, asking for help, went unanswered. In desperation, I asked the prison welfare officer to call my family on my behalf. It seemed no one was interested. I even got the prison chaplain to phone my sister Verina. He left a message on the answer machine. The next time he called her, the number had changed. It became clear that no one wished to associate or communicate with me. I had no home, no family or friends to talk to, no money, and no way out in sight.

Awakened to that fact, I had a moment of clarity. Humbly, I knelt on the cell floor and admitted to God and myself for the first time that I was a drug addicted alcoholic, and asked God, our creator, for help. I rose up from my knees to return to the sitting position on the single bed when a prison officer lifted the flap on the cell door, and asked, with eyes peering at me, "Would you like to go to an AA meeting?"

I thought it was something to do with the Automobile Association, and asked him, "What's it all about?"

"For people with alcoholic problems," he said. I realised God had answered my prayers, and immediately said: "Yes!" I had just practiced step one of the twelve steps of AA, NA and other fellowships, although I didn't know it at the time.

I was impressed by the honesty I heard at the meeting. I was also touched by Kelly the AA member who took time away from his wife and children, in order to assist in our recovery behind prison walls.

I began to awaken to the love of God, as I began to get in touch with my feelings, with no drugs or alcohol to hinder that process. I attended every meeting and was also introduced to the fellowship of Narcotics Anonymous (NA). I realised that I must have passed these fellowships as a suffering alcoholic drug addict many times, before and after losing my mind, home and dignity, while I engaged in crime for crack and alcohol. I had unwittingly passed many watering holes of recovery, as I battled with addiction.

Battle bruised and battered, but lucky and grateful to be alive, I asked social services for help via prison letters. They agreed to fund my treatment, and I agreed to go to St Luke's Rehab instead of Kairos, as it sounded more spiritual. I liaised with the CARAT drug and alcohol prison project for information and advice on recovery. I worked as a cleaner and on the hot plate, helping to feed and clothe my fellow inmates, and ensuring that the showers and toilets were kept clean.

As my release date approached, I expressed my anxiety about visiting the off-licence to the right of the prison. I knew I wouldn't make it to rehab once I had that celebratory drink. The AA secretary offered to meet me outside the prison, on my release. However, that arrangement was changed because my release date fell on a weekend. As a result, a man from the CARAT Team agreed to accompany me to rehab instead.

There was also a RAPT course for alcohol and drug rehabilitation, open to prisoners serving one year and upwards. By introducing fellow inmates to the fellowships of AA and NA, many prisoners managed to stay clean and sober on the outside or became humble and honest enough to ask for help. The only requirement for membership of an AA or NA fellowship is a desire to stop using.

Why didn't I simply carry on with abstinence from drugs and alcohol when I left prison, has remained a mystery to me. As we walked around the exercise yard in conversation, I told my fellow inmates about my forthcoming trip to rehab-ville. I was told St Luke's was one of the toughest rehabs in England, Scotland, Wales, and Ireland, and it would be like being transferred from one prison to another. After all these years of slowly committing suicide, I said I needed the discipline, and I was going there to obtain the keys to my freedom. At the time, I thought rehab would teach me how to drink and drug responsibly, like a gentleman, enabling me to competently manage all my affairs.

I conspired with others to carry out illegal transactions that would allow me to re-house myself in style, within a year. The fellowships asked for complete abstinence, but I thought rehab was different. I thought it was for the high-flying junkie, addict or alcoholic, who wants to hold on to what he's got, and accumulate more while continuing to use. That included relationships as well as business and material things. In the meantime, I accumulated brand-new prison jeans, shirts and T-shirts with HMP logos, with the intention of selling them to others. I was told I could get seventy pounds for a shirt and more for the jeans.

On arrival at reception at the beginning of the seven-month sentence I saw Zuti, a reliable supplier of quality coke and crack, who visited my apartment regularly.

He had pulled a gun out on me once, over one hundred and ten pounds that I owed him. Just as his respect had disappeared towards me, mine had also evaporated towards him, as I waited for him to pull the trigger, through the shadow of death, darkness and evil. For a man who liked the high life, and who was not short of money, it surprised me how cheaply he valued life, including his own. Who would want to go to prison for killing a man over one hundred and ten pounds? He didn't pull the trigger, and the gun went back into his pocket. I wasn't surprised to see him, since so many dealers and addicts were being admitted and released every day.

So, there we were, at prison reception together, the dealer and the addict. I soon discovered that he had smuggled in a large lump of crack. That got me excited. We ended up on the same wing and as a cleaner with the freedom to visit different landings, I visited his cell ASAP and scored some crack, using Virginia tobacco and phone cards as currency. The one hundred and ten pounds was never mentioned.

Although I was on duty as a cleaner, I immediately gave in to the obsessive compulsion to use. I sneaked into my cell for one hit on the plastic bottle crack pipe I'd made earlier. I'd just filled my lungs with crack smoke when a blonde lady prison officer came to my door. Before the door opened wide, the crack pipe was put out of sight, and I simply answered her by nodding my head. It was regarding my move to another landing, on the same wing.

As soon as she left, I exhaled amid anger, frustration and relief. I was angered by the prison officers timing, frustrated by the high that eluded me, but relieved about not being caught with the crack pipe. I took the incident as a sign that my crack smoking days were numbered, and I ought to call it a day. My resolve to attend rehab grew even stronger.

The inmate next door brewed hooch, but I turned it down. I was surprised and proud of myself, knowing that I actually said no to alcohol. Drug taking was rife on the wing, with inmates slipping into the landing toilets and showers, during association time, to have a boot of brown on the foil. As low and mad as I was, I thought they were crazy. I was surprised at the popularity and availability of brown (heroin) in prison. As a cleaner, and working on the hotplate, I had access to silver foil, which is a must-have accessory for an addict in prison. I stayed clear of the brown but used the foil for making crack pipes.

My love of ganja had been subdued by my obsession with crack, cocaine and alcohol. However, it became my number one habit within Wandsworth Prison walls. It was also cheaper and more accessible. In fact, good ganja was a real treat, as cannabis resin was readily available on every wing.

With rehab to look forward to and with my AA attendances in prison, I felt a sudden surge of hope, and believed that there was a light at the end of the tunnel, although I couldn't see it. All my overheated and conflicting emotions were still running wild, alongside countless defects of character. These included grandiose posturing, overweening pride, endless self-justification, denial and defiance. I was acutely oversensitive, childish and insecure. No matter how low down I was, I always managed to find myself looking down on others.

Chapter 18

Resurrection Time

I recalled my previous sentence, when I still had the flat in Putney. I thought I'd secured the place by applying for the rent to be paid by social security through the social services at HMP Wandsworth. Prior to that, I'd received notice of eviction, which I opposed. This resulted in a civil court case, scheduled for hearing during my sentence. Frantic phone calls to the court from myself and the prison service, followed. Even last-ditch letters from myself to the clerk of the court failed to get the hearing adjourned until after my release. The court ruling for eviction was ratified in my absence. The eviction date allowed me a month's stay before I had to vacate the premises.

I had hoped to launch an appeal on my release but failed to attend my solicitor's appointment because of my ongoing imprisonment and slavery to crack, cocaine and alcohol.

Before getting any knowledge of my eviction notice, I was in cell forty-two, on number 4 landing on E wing, when I felt a presence, an energy that passed through my cell. I responded spontaneously, by praying to God, asking him for Mamie to still be on earth on my release. On visiting my mum's house, I told her that Mamie would be my next stop on my way home. Surprised by my statement, Clive, my stepfather, asked me whether I had not been informed of Mamie's passing. I looked at him and Mama Jean in disbelief and asked Mama Jean for the location of Mamie's grave. My eyes swelled with tears. The world of Vander was completely demolished without warning.

It's a wonder I was still standing! My relationship with Mamie was, and still is, so deep and loving that I always believed I wouldn't be able to go on without her. The pain of not being informed about her passing was unbearable. At her sheltered accommodation, Mamie had said that out of all her grandchildren, it was she and I in the beginning, and it's the same thing at the end. She said that thirteen Alexander Court would be her last address on earth.

Mamie loved all her grandchildren unconditionally, whether they visited her or not. She comforted me in my pain and forgave me for stealing from her. I had yet to forgive myself. I stood there burning with guilt and shame, with grief and loss adding their intolerable weight. Lightning flashed, and thunder clapped and rolled through the dark clouds and recesses of my mind. In agony, my soul cried out! I felt Victoria Falls building inside me. Without another word, I rushed out of my mother's house. The dam that held back everything, burst as I reached the top of her drive. I cried out loud as water fell from my eyes. My next stop was the local off-licence. The shopkeeper refused to hand over the drink, because I was fifty pence short. In a rage, I demanded that he hand it over because I had to have it. He looked at me, relented, and handed me the drink.

Instead of heading for Mamie's, as previously planned, I returned to Putney in an empty carriage on the train, with tears streaming down my face with every gulp of alcohol. Suddenly, I heard Mamie's voice, as if from a million miles away. Her voice was distinct and clear, as I heard her say, "Don't worry. I'm happy! Where I am is better than heaven!" I cried even more after hearing those words. I told her that I missed her, yet deep within, I was grateful for our communication. Again, I was somehow comforted, as Mamie repeated the same words.

Now here I was, back serving another prison sentence, one of many that plagued the trail of my addiction. Prison was where my life went into replay, as I recalled such moments. Somehow, the loss of Mamie made me more determined to get well. The glimmer of hope grew, as my release date approached. It was encouraging to discover that one would get re-housed on completion of rehab. I continued to acquire new prison clothes, which I packed in black bin liners, ready for my release. When the day came, it felt strange not to be returning to the Putney flat. My life was in ruins but somehow, I felt different. The dynamics had changed. I had hope, whereas before, I had none.

I met Michael from the CARAT team at reception, and thankfully, handed him two black bin liners, full of prison clothes. I didn't reveal what was in the bags. The call from the off-licences to celebrate my release was muted that day. Michael's company made the difference. It gave me strength. He made a remark about how heavy the bags were, but I kept quiet and was quick to talk about something else. He was a guardian angel to me on that day. Thank you, Michael!

My life had truly taken a different course. I was on Recovery Street, instead of Demolition Drive. We travelled by bus, a far cry from the days when I was picked up by a fancy car or minicab outside the prison gates. From the prison reception, I arrived at St Luke's rehab reception, and thanked Michael for his support. Years later, I'm still incredibly appreciative and grateful for where his support has helped to take me. After a warm and bright reception, I was shown to my room, and was visited there almost immediately by Muriel, the counsellor, a lovely, dapperly dressed little lady, and sharp as a laser beam.

She asked me to empty the contents of the black bin bags. Then she looked at me in astonishment, as all the prison jeans, shirts, t-shirts, and prison issue steel toe capped boots, were revealed.

She asked me, "Why have you got so much prison clothing in your possession, Vander?" "I'm keeping some for myself, and I'm going to sell the rest to make some money, because I'm broke," I replied. "That's theft, and you'll have to return all the prison clothes," she said. "Furthermore, you're in rehab now, and you have to be honest to recover," she added. She gently encouraged me to begin to let go of my old way of life and to change my thinking.

I looked at her in disbelief and said, "You must be joking!" She was serious alright. I had an urge to laugh, but couldn't, as I'd lost my sense of humour. I hadn't laughed for years. My face had turned to stone. To laugh again would be a dream come true, a miracle! I had a little room, with a little bed, and a little wardrobe. It was better than being homeless and infinitely better than living in a crack house. Spiritually, mentally, emotionally, materially and financially ruined, I felt vulnerable, humbled, and willing to learn. With nowhere to go, I felt I had no choice but to stay, no matter what.

There were over thirty residents at St Luke's. I made my acquaintance, first with those I met in the lounge before lunch, and then was introduced to all my peers in the group therapy that followed. I was disappointed with the selection of women, except for one I saw on my admittance at reception. I thought she worked there, until I spoke to her in the lounge after making my acquaintance with Muriel, with whom I had my first reality check. In group therapy, the counsellor encouraged all of us to be honest, and take risks, by pouring out our hearts and minds. We were to embrace this opportunity and dump as much rubbish as we could find within ourselves, so we'd leave rehab a lighter and better person.

Suddenly it was a "we" thing and not a "me" thing. We were there to support each other, in our common goal to recover from addiction. We were there to offload all the things that caused our feelings of guilt, anger and resentment. We were to face our fears and speak, even if it might offend someone else. We were as sick as our secrets, and people pleasing was out.

Many of my peers couldn't identify their feelings from the feelings chart, not knowing whether they felt anxious, or fearful. Identifying my feelings was no problem. However, living with them, and managing them, without drugs and alcohol, was impossible. I attended an AA meeting that evening after tea. We were allowed to go out in groups. That way we kept safe, especially in our first month in rehab. I was determined to be a different man in three months' time, better than the one who came in.

I met Charles, my counsellor, the next day, a tall black man with an athletic build, wearing round silver metal-framed glasses that made him look like a young professor. I thought Muriel was going to be my counsellor. I wondered if she'd passed me onto Charles, thinking I'd be too much hard work, after making such a dishonest start with all that HMP clobber. Charles told me that my first assignment would be to write my life story, which I'd have to read to my peers. He encouraged me to be truthful and courageous in what I wrote, in our scheduled one-to-one sessions as well as in group therapy. I also discovered that Charles was a recovering addict just like us and attended meetings in the East End.

I was given my cleaning duties by the team leader at the time. We were all allocated cleaning duties. Arrangements for health checks were made under the direction of the rehab. I wasn't allowed any phone-calls for one month, and my mobile was put into storage. One month without receiving or making phone-calls didn't bother me at all. The only people who could possibly call me were drug dealers.

Charles told me not to worry about money, and to just focus on my recovery. He said that I could leave the building at any time, so there was no need to sneak out the window and climb over the six-foot white wall at night. This was a no-nonsense rehab and any relapse in drink and drug taking would result in an immediate discharge. There was also random drug testing. St Luke's policy was based on a twelve-step programme and Charles advised me to attend AA and NA, as one focused on alcohol, and the other, on drugs. We had to attend a minimum of three meetings a week. I enjoyed the meetings and went every day. I was inspired, strengthened and given hope by what I heard from other alcoholics and drug addicts.

Not only had many recovered from a hopeless state, spiritually, mentally and physically, but they'd also been reunited with family, friends, jobs and homes they'd lost. Many had gained degrees as well as professional qualifications. They were going on holidays and had money in the bank. Others had resurrected careers as musicians, singers, writers, actors, comedians, models, and lawyers. Many were counsellors or working in other areas in recovery.

143

That also included the businessmen, who'd bounced back after being written off.

Returning the prison clothes to HMP Wandsworth was a humbling experience, yet I still harboured thoughts of connecting with gangsters who would help me amass large sums of money. That way, I'd quickly reclaim my self-respect, and trappings of wealth. However, financial wealth can be a trap, just like drugs and alcohol, and I now know that true self-respect can only be earned, not bought.

Group therapy was headed by various counsellors, and we all had our favourites. Most people in therapy still had their families, friends, jobs, homes and bank accounts. Some people would burst into tears during group sessions, but I found it difficult to empathise with them, as I wondered what on earth were they crying for! Look at me! I'd lost everything. Suddenly, I registered the fact that I had life and that couldn't be bought.

At that stage, I didn't understand that addiction is a mental illness, for which there's no known cure, and that their rock bottoms, even with jobs, families, friends, homes, finance and romance intact, were still just as painful to them as my plight was to me. They'd gotten out of the descending lift of addiction on the sixth, fifth and fourth floor. As for me, I'd gone to the basement, and just to get to the ground floor would be a miracle. Most addicts and alcoholics who go to the basement, the point of no return, go on to the bitter end. It was only by the grace of God that I managed to ascend to the ground floor.

I began to recognise various characters and personalities in groups. Those who said nothing, those who kept crying, those who were angry, and those who were frightened. There was a lot of guilt, regret and remorse. At the same time, there was a lot of pretention. But in all this, there was, above all, the healing process, as one embarked on a spiritual journey.

Despite all the denial, defiance and selfishness, there were dried sticks that miraculously began to bud, leaf and flower before my very eyes. It was always made manifest with humility, honesty, and acceptance of life on life's terms. It was, and still is, a privilege, pleasure, and an honour, to witness and be part of that process. We were discouraged from wearing clothing that advertised or glorified alcohol, drugs and immorality in any way. Muriel and Charles were both keen to point out the need to let go of the gangster walk and talk. They said that such behaviour could lead me back to hell, that dreaded place that I had determined would never claim me back again.

In my first one-to-one with Charles, he swiftly indicated that I had anger and abandonment issues. The abandonment issues were traced back to when my mother and father left me in Mamie's care, to go to England. I denied that I had any such issues. I said my parents went to England to prepare what they believed would be a better start for their children.

When I mentally revisited the jetty, from which my mum and dad stepped down into a rowing boat, before they disappeared inside the big ship, my words to my mother, "I'll find you even if I have to walk across the sea," made me realise that I was truly traumatised by this parting from her, although it wasn't permanent. I didn't remember anything concerning my father at the time.

With my new-found willingness to be honest, open-minded, and to do the right thing, I confessed my anger, while remaining cool and calm on the surface. Yes, I was angry at being homeless, angry at being financially broke, angry at being estranged from my family and friends, angry with society, angry for being defeated by drugs and alcohol, angry at losing all my possessions, angry for losing my self-respect, angry for losing my dignity, angry for losing my mind, angry with myself, and angry with the world. I was told that the people who cried in groups were getting in touch with their feelings, and that's a big breakthrough in recovery. I wasn't ready to cry in front of people. Instead, I did my best to remain like a stone. Thank God I never succeeded.

I was buoyant, humbled, and full of hope, after that one-to-one session with Charles. Now, I had to complete my life story. Charles told me to ensure that I give an honest account. I assured him that I would. Apart from experiencing what I now know to be a spiritual void, I also felt like a coiled spring, ready to unleash at any moment. I was angry, I was a walking time bomb, as if I was still in active addiction. I hoped to leave that person behind after three months and recover my true being.

Charles assured me that I was on a path of change, and that as long as I was true to myself, that change would eventually happen. He said his door was always open to me. I thanked him and returned to a lounge that was in need of refurbishment.

I scanned the notice board on the wall to determine what meeting I'd attend that evening. We had a good chef and I always looked forward to mealtimes, and the huge bowls of fruits that were there for our benefit. Charles, Muriel and the other counsellors were right. This was a spiritual place, and what was hidden in the dark had a way of emerging into the light.

I witnessed that every day. I heard about child abuse, infidelity, thefts from workplaces, and so much more. There were other forms of dishonesty as well. During one group session, Fabio said that I had intimidated him into lending me ten pounds. I looked at Charles, my counsellor, and said that it was an absolute lie. I thought Fabio and I were friends. Furthermore, I said I wouldn't demand money with threats, with an intention to repay that money at the same time! Others in the group backed Fabio. This began to look like a black and white thing, a conspiracy to sabotage my recovery. You could get evicted for behaving like that.

Somehow Fabio and his backers weren't as convincing, as it appeared that they'd formed a clique, both in and out of groups. Incidentally, the woman I first saw at reception on my arrival was part of that clique, and believed I was jealous of her closeness to a more recent admission. I wasn't jealous at all. We had never kissed, held hands, had coffee or walks in the park together. Suddenly, the word insanity came to mind. Here we were, all sick people, seeking to get well, but I didn't quite see it like that at the time. I was seething with rage but managed to maintain my composure.

At the next group session, the new arrival sprung from his chair, spoiling for a fight, and accused me of talking about him, behind his back, to my counsellor concerning his relationship with the said female. There were no secrets in there. Their relationship was apparent for all to see. We were all under a microscope, and nothing stayed secret. There were evictions. People who I thought were doing well, were evicted for drinking alcohol. Others simply failed to return after a visit to the bank, to withdraw money they'd been waiting on.

I was still anticipating some state benefits and felt small without any money. My prison discharge grant had expired weeks ago. It seemed that I was the only one in rehab without finance. Letters I wrote for assistance were ignored. That really hurt, as it took a great effort to ask for help.

Chapter 19

Taking Stock

As I sank into despair, I remembered Charles' words, "Don't worry about money, recovery isn't about external things". They were true. There were lots of suffering addicts and alcoholics with all the trappings of wealth, who still appeared to be in more pain than me. I took stock, and began to be thankful for the food, shelter, and clothes on my back.

Writing my life-story brought up countless painful emotions, as I recalled the harm that I had I inflicted on others and myself. I had put crack, cocaine and alcohol before God, myself, family and friends, and society. I had put alcohol and drugs before life itself, and that was an excruciating experience.

I remembered the bus driver who'd stop by a crack house on Garratt Lane in Wandsworth, with the bus parked outside, with passengers on board. He'd leave an hour later, with the remaining passengers totally oblivious to his misdeeds. I don't know how he managed to return to duty after smoking crack. If that had been me, the bus would've remained parked outside. I reflected on the danger that an addict-alcoholic poses to himself and the general public.

I remembered being on bail to Oxford Crown Court, charged with smuggling over two hundred thousand pounds worth of sensimilla. That charge came about through guilt by association. I wasn't in possession of any ganja nor were there any statements made against me. I remember the acute anxiety I had felt, as I imagined my sons and daughters waiting in vain for me to turn up, time and time again. God only knows what I put them through.

I even failed to show up to the weddings of my brother and two sisters, as a result of substance abuse. I don't even know how I managed to sign on at the police station when I was on bail for that smuggling charge. I was always high on my drugs of choice when I gave them my signature. The bottom line was: I knew failing to sign on would have resulted in my arrest and an unwelcome interruption of my habit.

Failure to see my children left me free to continue my self-abuse. But of course, I could never be free from the pain of my irresponsibility. It continued to consume me. I revisited those suicidal thoughts, and don't know how I concluded that I needed to increase my consumption of drugs and alcohol in order to keep those thoughts at bay. That was the answer to every situation in life, whether times were good or not so good. Everything became a reason to use. As I wrote my life story down, I began to see addiction as a cunning and callous enemy of life.

Leaving my grandmother without the wherewithal to buy food, after stealing her money, caused me to sink even further in a mire of pain that became the prison in which I existed. Even the shoes and clothes I wore turned to pain! The pain was within and without, and the catalogue of destruction is something that I could write about, for years to come. However, I had to bring my life story to a conclusion since I was determined to deliver it on time. Failure to deliver assignments or attend groups on time would be met with a warning, penalties, and ultimately, eviction. The same applied for breaking any house rules.

I baulked at the thought of putting certain things on paper, as they tended to glorify crime and addiction. Charles said, "Write it, as long as it is true," and so I did! This included revelations of the copious amounts of crack, cocaine and alcohol I took. Others who had taken less were no longer with us. The constant bottles of champagne, and cognac, money stashed around the house and other addresses, the earthenware pot full of cocaine for personal use, and the entourage of three to four cars full of shady male characters that followed my lead into the nightclubs or to the recording studios, all seemed glamorous on paper, but in reality, there was the fear of being burgled, robbed, conned, informed on, arrested, murdered, or committing a murder. Fear of losing my girlfriend was a big one for me, although she could easily be replaced.

I said I never feared anyone, including the police or prison. But in reality, I was riddled with fear. Those feelings of fear were at the centre of my addiction. Fear manifested its myriad forms through defects of character, which I've mentioned earlier, time and time again. This included intolerance, 'judgementalism', control and manipulation. Fear of not getting something or fear of losing something, contaminated nearly every area in my life.

Vanities, false promises, delusions, illusions, confusion, dishonesty, people pleasing, character assassination, grandiosity, emotional, mental and financial insecurities, doubt, lack of trust, procrastination, self-justification, pride and jealousy all came from a state of fear, but I didn't know it at the time.

In the midst of writing my life story, I decided to adopt all the counsellors as my aunts and uncles. My peers became my brothers and sisters, and the people I met at the fellowships of AA and NA became my extended family.

St Luke's was a spiritual place. I felt the love and care that emanated from the counsellors, and beheld the progress being made by my peers and me. For example, every day, some in the groups who never spoke up previously were suddenly opening up. I saw tears from others turn to laughter. Some who intended to leave, decided to stay, and there was a lot of love, good advice, encouragement and inspiration in both the fellowships. I didn't feel so alone anymore and began to trust the process.

I handed my life story to Charles a fortnight later. The next day when I saw him, he looked at me with searching eyes, as if he questioned the authenticity of what I wrote; the lavish lifestyle I had lived before my descent into crack houses, petty crime, imprisonment and eviction that had brought me here.

"It's all true," I said. "Then we'll leave it as it is," he replied. Even now, as I sit here writing this book, I remember stuff that I didn't mention in my life story. Like the time I visited my friend Errol with a large plastic bag of cocaine. His lovely girlfriend Angie, who smoked crack, was heavily pregnant. I made it clear to him that I had no intention of sharing any of my cocaine with his girlfriend, who was upstairs at the time. I urged him not to give her any, for obvious reasons. He agreed but found himself creeping upstairs to feed her habit. I felt ill at ease, and disappointed with his behaviour. Then out of the eerie silence, a cry came from Angie, exclaiming that she was in labour. In a panic, he rushed to drive her to the maternity ward.

I was left alone in the house and continued to feed my habit. But the delivery and health of that baby played on my mind. I couldn't get high, no matter how much I smoked. Errol returned a few hours later, wearing a long face, uttering the word, "stillborn". He had just seen his dead son, who was like an image of himself. Disgust erupted inside me. I felt that I'd been instrumental in this tragic loss of life! The fact that I was against giving her any crack was of no consolation. I immediately tied a knot on the bag of coke, picked up my pipe, and started to leave. Errol pleaded with me to leave him some coke. I declined, and with the words, "I told you!" I left his house. I didn't see him again until a few years later.

As in most crack-infected relationships, Errol's and Angie's didn't last much longer, although they'd been happy together for years before crack and cocaine came and devastated their lives. While writing my autobiography, I discovered that Angie is no longer with us and Errol is still married to the crack pipe.

Well, the day came to open myself up to my peers with my life story, with my counsellor supervising the group. My peers were very receptive and thanked me for my truth. My lifestyle was a far cry from most of theirs. However, we had a lot of similarities when it came to the obsession, compulsion, and consequences of addiction. In order to get well, we were advised to focus on the similarities and not the differences in our life stories. I felt some order coming into my life, as I submitted to the rehab routine.

I wrote a poem entitled 'Alcoholic', which Charles said ought to go up on the notice board, and it goes like this:

I woke up in the morning
Craving for a drink
Reached out for the alcohol
Instead of the bathroom sink
Drank plenty water with raw lemons
And ate a lot of garlic to detoxify
My heart said you're an alcoholic
My mind said no, it's a lie.

Rehab arranged for me to have a blood test in order to determine my state of health. It revealed that I was in remarkably good health considering the abuse that my body and brain had suffered. I was relieved that my health would not be added to my long list of losses.

Many of my male peers had great difficulty sleeping at nights, and would congregate by the kettle room, drinking copious amounts of tea and coffee. Didn't they know that coffee kept them awake? Looking back, I realised that they were probably fixing on caffeine, whilst missing their girlfriends and wives. Occasionally, I would join them after a trip to the loo, at two or three a.m. While they missed their girlfriends and wives, I missed having money, and a home to go to at the end of my three-month stay.

More one-to-ones with Charles revealed to me how my fear of abandonment and rejection as a child made me reluctant about asking for help and played a big part in sabotaging my relationships with women. Anytime I entered a steady relationship with a woman, I'd wonder just how long it would last. It transpired that my steady relationships all had a shelf life of four years and that included my marriage. As a result, I held a secret desire to better that, and still do.

Michael, from the CARAT team at HMP Wandsworth, assured me that he'd visit my flat, and secure some of my belongings. I hoped that he would secure some of my Savile Row suits, with a few pairs of crocodile shoes as well as a beautiful batik and a mystical oil painting of mine. He turned up at the rehab with a framed and signed picture of Steel Pulse and some knick-knacks, which I didn't really care for and I still don't remember what they were. I was gutted, but thanked him all the same, while masking my disappointment.

Charles spent most of his time with other clients, whom I believe he felt were more vulnerable than myself. One of them was Kate, who had an infant daughter and was married to a rich man. She wouldn't stop crying in group-meetings. She took up most of his time, he seemed to be on a mission to save her marriage.

Another assignment of mine was naming the triggers that could cause me to relapse. After much soul-searching, the only answer I came up with was bereavement in the family.

I still harboured thoughts of making a quick and substantial sum of money after my discharge. On my way to a fellowship meeting one evening, I met Lewis, a gangster acquaintance of mine. He'd served seven years for conspiracy to import cocaine into England and spent the bulk of his sentence in HMP Wandsworth. I assured him that I would be in touch in a matter of weeks. Shame and embarrassment prevented me from letting him know that I was in rehab and on my way to an NA or AA meeting at the time.

Chapter 20
A Higher Purpose

In my next one-to-one, Charles stressed how imperative it was that I leave my criminal associations behind and avoid all the haunts that I'd frequented in the past. Otherwise, my chances of recovery would be short-lived. He discouraged me from believing everything I heard in the fellowships. Although it was an honest programme, he said those fellowships were like society in miniature. They harboured thieves, drug pushers, sex offenders, liars and all sorts as well as the ones on the straight and narrow.

"Vander, your thinking has to change, or else you'll return to active addiction!" he exclaimed. I wondered if he could read my mind and asked him, "Are you telepathic?" Charles replied, "Why the questions?" I remained silent, instead of revealing my criminal plans to return to financial prosperity. My belief in the spirituality of St Luke's began to deepen as I felt God had spoken to me through Charles.

Research into telepathy was my final excuse for drinking and drugging, as the older excuses that ended with "this will be my last indulgence, and tomorrow will be different," didn't hold water anymore.

I believed in telepathy and believed that crack and cocaine enhanced my telepathic powers. During those coke and crack sessions, I'd focus on various women, and mentally ask them to visit me at my place for sex. I'd go to my window, to see if the car that pulled up outside contained the sexy body that would satisfy my lust. They never ever turned up. Who would at four a.m.? My preoccupation with telepathy proved to be the most expensive research I had ever done. It had cost me seventeen arrests, twelve short prison sentences, and homelessness. However, I still believe in telepathy today. I just went about it in a deluded way.

We embarked on a twelve-step programme in groups. The first step was admitting that we were powerless over our addiction and that our lives had become unmanageable. So much of my life had been demolished within and without. I accepted step one absolutely. Others in the group struggled with that, especially the unmanageability aspect. They were the ones who still had family, homes, jobs and money in the bank. Then why were they in rehab? They eventually relented, as soon as they realised how close they had come to losing those things.

With step two, we came to believe that a power greater than ourselves could restore us to sanity. I believed in a power greater than myself, but I didn't think I was insane. It wasn't until the counsellor pointed out that insanity was repeating the same things over and over again and expecting a different result that made me let go of that erroneous belief. I felt as if I was waking up. Most of my peers accepted that but some were in doubt, or denial, as they had no belief in a power greater than themselves.

Step three was making a decision to turn our will and our lives over to the care of God, as we understood him. St Luke's and the fellowships identified that God as a loving God. God was no longer demonised as being full of wrath, sending all transgressors into a pit of fire. Some of my peers chose the spirits of their ancestors as their God or higher power, which was helping and comforting them in their distress. Others chose the power of nature: the sun, the moon and stars, earth, wind, fire, water, even the trees. Some made their girlfriends and boyfriends their higher power, a big mistake that proved painful to so many, as the frailties and limits of the human condition gradually revealed themselves, causing many to relapse in the process. There were those whose higher power started off as a toothbrush, cat or dog, and eventually progressed to a belief in God as a Great Spirit, source and creator of all life.

I accepted all the steps and felt that I'd come home, as I embarked on this spiritual journey and way of life. I thanked Mamie in my heart, for introducing me to God and prayer as an infant. I woke up to the fact that it was my free will that got me into difficulties and God was, and always would be there, to give me victory as soon as I turned my will and my life over to him. Instead of taking control, I relinquished all control to God. God is love and life!

Accepting life on life's terms was, and still is, crucial to my recovery. Without humility, I was going nowhere. I learned through the fellowships that there's no graduation in spirituality, and that what kept me clean and sober yesterday, wouldn't keep me clean and sober today. I only had a daily reprieve and would start afresh every day, turning my will and my life over to the care of God, a God full of love, mercy and compassion, a God who never abandons or fails us as humans do. It was I who'd abandoned him.

Difficulties became opportunities to invite God into my life. They would help me grow spiritually, mentally and emotionally. Difficulties were there to strengthen my faith, not weaken it.

One day, Charles questioned me about the phone calls I was receiving from a lady-friend I met at the Eaton Square meeting in Belgravia. The payphone at the foot of the staircase was being monitored, and I felt it was an invasion of privacy. I changed my tune, as I came to understand that this was in aid of our recovery. It was recommended that we refrain from getting into a relationship, for at least one year, as there were so many emotional relapses in the early stages of recovery. This was echoed by some of the disastrous stories I heard from my peers in rehab as well as in the fellowships. I cooled off my communication with Anne and focused on my recovery. It wasn't easy.

I enjoyed the meditation and relaxation groups as well as nearly every other group session. In the ones with confrontations, I learned to deal with my feelings, and began to grow by being assertive, instead of being aggressive, or submissive.

Submission was to God, to life, and to the twelve steps in the fellowships. Rehab and the fellowships taught me that surrender to the truth about addiction, and to God and life, made me a winner.

I went into rehab thinking that I was going to learn to drink and smoke drugs like a gentleman. I imagined that I could resume my criminal connections, buy a house within a year, and still continue producing songs.

Abstinence from all drugs was difficult to accept, and placing boundaries on people, places and things I usually associated with, made it a monumental task. To drive in the slow lane filled me with fear, frustration and anxiety, as I wanted everything now and not tomorrow. I still hadn't received any money.

Charles said, "Don't worry, use this opportunity to discard as much of the old self, as is possible". "It's alright for you to say that with money in your pocket, a home, a job you like, and a lovely girlfriend!" I thought. I kept it to myself. Furthermore, he was right: I had food, clothes and shelter; the money would come eventually. Charles questioned my pretensions as he noticed that I attended a lot of meetings in Belgravia. "I enjoy uptown and downtown meetings," was my reply.

It felt good to become a senior member amongst my peers. Recovery was about being honest, open-minded and willing. I noticed a shift within myself in that direction. I also began to notice it amongst my peers.

Breaking into tears is considered a breakthrough in rehab, and my turn came when I spoke about stealing my Mamie's money and pension book, knowing that she relied on that money for her weekly food shopping and to pay her bills. It was like a tsunami when it came, as it rose out of nowhere. My self-will was overwhelmed by a flood of tears. I went with the flow. Everyone was speechless. All I could hear was myself, crying in pain. Yes! I felt as if I'd made a breakthrough as I wiped my face with the industrial tissue paper that sat in abundance in the Discovery Room. All, our group-meeting rooms had positive names. There was a

Reflection room as well. What my peers thought of me now didn't bother me like I thought it would.

In fact, some alpha males, and wannabe gangsters, some females too, privately confided in me that they'd love to cry, and soon after, some of them did. A hardened heart, steeped in anger and fear, had kept me using. A soft heart, conceived in truth, love, compassion and forgiveness, was keeping me clean and sober, one day at a time. What a revelation! The time came to collect my money from the post office and Charles insisted that I be accompanied by one of my peers. I felt insulted and angry at the suggestion. My discharge was due that same month.

I thought this action showed his lack of confidence in me. "Don't you trust me?" I asked.

"Yes, I do. However, it's the addict in you that I don't trust!" Charles exclaimed. It made sense. It showed that he cared. The disease of addiction was in me. Sheer ego was trying to lead me into isolation, and once on my own, I could sabotage my recovery. In retrospect, that was a possibility that I could ill afford. I had to hand in the money on my return to rehab and had to ask Charles' permission to spend it and explain what I needed it for.

St Luke's, with its Spartan conditions, was a tough place but it was heaven after living in a crack house. My forwarding address was Bolingbroke, which was the second stage of St Luke's recovery programme. All being well, I'd eventually be re-housed from there.

It was a big beautiful house near Clapham Common, and my room was large and luxurious. Staff occupied the ground floor, in an office-type environment, and were absent at nights and on weekends.

They were relatively few in number but there to give us support. All the residents, to my disappointment, were male. Still, it felt like I was going up in the world. I attended foot-massaging sessions with a visiting masseuse. Eating my meals at a banqueting table in the dining room made me feel like a king. I got on with the two male residents, who appeared to be enjoying their stay, and they were full of praise and gratitude for St Luke's and the Bolingbroke staff, as they vocally reflected on the gutter from whence they came. I totally identified!

The kitchen was massive, and well equipped, and I looked forward to expressing my culinary skills. The female staff worked with us to ensure that we ate healthily. The back garden was large and lovely, with a big and beautiful tree as well as shrubs, herbs, and flowers. I joyfully watered the garden, as I gravitated towards nature in the radiant sunshine.

My discharge from St Luke's had been an emotional affair. I was presented with a book on the 'Twelve Steps of Recovery' that was signed with good wishes from my peers. We were in the Discovery Room again, as each peer gave a farewell speech. I was moved by the love that I discovered that day, and humbly thanked them as I wished them all a strong and happy recovery. Time and time again, we'd been told that only three to four of us, out of thirty-four, would successfully recover. I wondered which of us were the fortunate few. It was the second- and third-time round for some of my peers.

In fact, Leila, who came to St Luke's some weeks after me, disappeared after being entrusted to go on her own to collect her state benefit from the post office. Apparently, she ended up in a Brixton crack house and proceeded to the West End, where things got even worse. She returned to St Luke's before I left, humbled by her experience, willing to listen and learn, whereas she'd been defiant before.

Well, here I was in Bolingbroke, so far so good. I had a feeling of discomfort and couldn't understand why, as I was in a lovely house with lovely people, clean and sober. I thought about those people who drank aftershave because of the alcohol content. I was glad I wasn't feeling like that. In fact, I was shocked when I first heard my peers confess to drinking aftershave. No wonder St Luke's prohibited all aftershaves, colognes and perfumes!

Although it wasn't like that at Bolingbroke, there was a camera that observed all our comings and goings, even at weekends. Around five weeks passed with regular meetings with both fellowships. I reflected on St Luke's and remembered the day that I left the dining room, wondering what was I going to do with my life, as my old behaviour was no longer an option. It was at that moment that Charles came along the corridor from the opposite direction, looked at me, and exclaimed, "Vander, you can achieve anything, as long as you're clean and sober!" Again, I thought God had spoken through him. I wondered if he was telepathic. I immediately decided to return to the music business. I had to be true to my heart instead of choosing an easier option that paid the bills.

Chapter 21

In a Dangerous Place

I decided to go and retrieve my bag of songs, poetry and a novel that I had started when I was at Mamie's. I'd sworn that I'd never drink or smoke crack again, but I was going to a dangerous place, a family home that had turned into a crack house. I had to retrieve my work, yet my instincts told me to leave it alone and start writing afresh. I considered asking someone to accompany me but shelved the idea. I'd simply go to Wembley, ring Prem's bell, ask for my bag of songs, declare that I no longer drink and smoke, and leave instantly.

I arrived at Prem's house on a glorious sunny Sunday afternoon. I had already agreed to greet clients at an NA meeting at Horseferry Road that evening, at seven p.m. I was overconfident. Prem said that he didn't have the bag of songs and excused himself to go into the backroom, while I waited in the front room for him to return from the crack pipe, so I could wish him goodbye.

"Vander come!" Prem exclaimed from the back. I entered the backroom, with heavy curtains drawn on a sunny day. He handed me a Martel miniature bottle crack pipe. I took it without saying a word and as soon as I exhaled, I felt guilt, shame and regret. I drank some alcohol to help me come down. I thought about my commitment, and became fearful of attending the meeting, smelling of alcohol on a crack come down. I managed to leave before things got any worse, and headed for Horseferry Road, feeling depressed and deflated. I was in a state of paranoia as I greeted other members of the fellowship, wondering if they could tell that I'd been on the pipe. "The only requirement for membership is a desire to stop using." I'd used! But I still had a desire to stop.

This was an opportunity to share the incident with my fellows, and free myself from guilt, shame, regret and anger, but I did no such thing. I suffered in silence and became as sick as my secrets.

Instead of heading to Bolingbroke after the meeting, I headed straight to Brixton, scored some crack, and proceeded to my room in Clapham Common. I smoked it and found myself leaving the building after midnight to score more. I didn't care about the camera that recorded my comings and goings. I sprayed my room with aftershave to disguise the crack fumes. I felt that I'd betrayed the residents and staff. I felt that I'd betrayed myself. This was a zero-tolerance house and eviction was imminent if I was found out. I had to get the crack out of my system. I drank lots of vinegar and lemon juice and water. I went about the house in fear and suspense.

Tuesday morning saw me being called for a urine sample. It proved positive. I had to leave immediately. Dawn, the lovely lady of Bolingbroke, had turned to stone. I was out of the building in less than an hour, with two black bin liners containing all I possessed. Brother J, who resided in the room next door, shook his head in disbelief at how crazy I'd been. "Why did you do it?" he asked. I said nothing. I'd sabotaged my recovery, and there I was, waiting for a bus, standing opposite the house from where I'd just been evicted. I felt that I had been dealt with harshly by what was supposed to be a caring profession.

I arrived at Wandsworth homeless person's unit and handed them the letter from Bolingbroke. I waited. Although I'd relapsed, I wasn't the same person that went into rehab.

I was allocated to Emscote Hotel in Balham. My hope of decent accommodation was denied, as I discovered that Emscote Hotel was nothing more than a health and safety hazard awaiting demolition.

My room made prison cells I'd known seem luxurious. The manager was an ex-lifer, who always wore dark glasses. Emscote Hotel was the pits, and the dregs of the earth were sent there. The place was plagued with alcoholics, drug addicts, thieves and prostitutes. There were also decent couples with their babies, but that was a minority. Doors were locked after midnight, and it was a hell of a job to get in after that hour.

I became acquainted with a crack dealer who supplied the building. Ray, the manager, didn't care for crack, although he was a chronic alcoholic. He was what you called a functioning alcoholic. Guys like him were clearly ignorant of the fact that alcohol is a drug. I befriended a well-mannered Trinidadian man, by the name of Brian, who never ran out of strong lager and bottles of vodka. My resolve to stay clean and sober had diminished greatly in the conditions I found myself in. I was surprised that the council sent me there, as the letter from Bolingbroke was evidence that I was in recovery and vulnerable.

Soon, I found myself shoplifting and selling garden shrub, chopped up and wrapped in cling film, to unsuspecting drunks during pub hours. I was in pain again. I had to get back on track. I visited the social services at St George's hospital at Tooting Broadway. I asked George for help, but he wasn't sure that I wanted another shot at rehab. I walked there and back to Emscote Hotel a few more times before George became convinced. He knew about the inhospitable conditions in which I was living. He was also shocked that Wandsworth council sent me there and was surprised that the place was still standing. It wasn't a place where you would invite anyone back for tea or coffee.

With George on my side, I got the funding, and ended up in St Augustine's rehab in Camden Town, six weeks later. They didn't have a twelve-step programme but insisted that we attend AA and NA meetings. There was a homely feel to this rehab in St Augustine's road, and I was given the lovely Miriam as my counsellor. I preferred my counsellor to be a former addict. Fortunately, I was a recovering addict and so was Miriam. She had a reputation for being cold, but I only saw her as a woman, doing the best she could. Before admitting me into St Augustine's, Miriam gave me a drug test. She found traces of cocaine but said it was low enough for me to be admitted.

I felt more at home there than at Bolingbroke. I was to spend six months there, as my first and second stage in rehab. They were more flexible and compassionate, willing to give you a chance. However, I was grateful for all I had learned at St Luke's as it enhanced my performance at St Augustine's. This rehab had about eleven clients and five members of staff. It wasn't luxurious like Bolingbroke, but I was grateful to be there.

The end of my stay at Emscote Hell (not hotel) had found me searching the back of Sainsbury's, Tesco and Asda, for thrown out, expired food. I thought I was being smart and resourceful since it enabled me to keep all my money for crack and alcohol. That's how my relapse came about so quickly. They said at St Luke's that when you return to active addiction, you don't start all over again, but pick up from where you left off, and it's true. Just walking upstairs took so much effort. That was something I'd never experienced before.

We lived more like tenants in St Augustine's, cooking our own meals, sharing the kitchen and dining area with staff. There was even a garden, albeit a small one, for such a large house.

Angie, one of our peers in St Augustine's, was in rehab for the eighth time. I couldn't believe it. After all the stress and strain I went through, just to get a second admission. She must be addicted to rehab, I thought. John from Hackney said he felt no guilt, shame, remorse or regret in groups, and after a month of maintaining that stance, he was asked to leave, as he wasn't considered ready for rehab. Another woman, who had recently arrived, was there in a bid to keep custody of her little son. She relapsed within a fortnight and chose to leave rather than accept a second chance.

Being a witness to the callous destruction of self and others made me shake my head in resignation at our powerlessness over drugs and alcohol, and how they made our lives unmanageable. There was tearful and quiet Maggie, who Angie manipulated and controlled, as if it were a rescue mission. There were Janet and Jed, from up north. They weren't a couple, but they soon began to act like one. Jed had been living rough on the streets for years and was considered a lost cause until a social worker had taken a special interest in him. He was allowed to get more upset and feistier than anyone else, in or out of the groups. When he lifted a chair and threatened Janet with it, he was allowed to stay. If that had been anyone else, they'd have had to go.

It was a delight to see so many people suddenly regaining their health. They were getting sets of teeth where there were none, getting glasses to ease the stress on their eyes, getting treatment for Hepatitis and other health issues due to drug and alcohol abuse. St Augustine's was in the midst of an area of prolific drug dealing, a stone's throw away from Camden Town Tube Station.

I prayed as I walked through that route to meetings. I avoided it as much as possible, as I saw lumps of crack spat out of mouths in street deals. Being attracted to such behaviour meant I was still sick, although I had a desire to stop using.

As I stood at a bus stop by Camden Road over-ground railway station, a regular face on the turf at the time, handed me a ten-pound bone of crack. I looked at it in his hand, then looked at him, and said, "No thanks!" "Take it, I'm giving it to you, not selling it!" he replied. "Thanks, but I don't smoke it anymore," I answered. He moved on in disbelief as my bus came along. I shared that experience in the group. It felt good to say no to drugs. It was an empowering experience. Why didn't dealers offer me crack for free when I was using? Street dealers (shotters) didn't offer free crack at bus stops. That was a clear demonstration of the guile of the dealer in his efforts to recapture your soul and the tenacity of the disease of addiction.

I had to be vigilant and live in the present moment every day. "Never" became a word that I was reluctant to use, unless I added God's name to it.

I found myself as the only one using the word God. The others feared or hated God for one reason or another. I discovered a lot of people were afraid of the word God, because confessing belief would not look rational or cool.

The rehab ran in similar ways to St Luke's when it came to group therapy. I had to write my life story again, and in doing so, it conjured up more memories. Like when I met Wolfie in HMP Wandsworth reception area, singing about the virtues of leaving crack cocaine alone, "Brother you're right, crack is a destruction to humanity," I said. He looked at me, sighed, and said he was serving a life sentence for killing his friend, over a ten-pound bone. That friend was the cousin of a well-known celebrity.

Then I remembered the Yardie who threatened his friends with a gun because he wanted the last bit of crack for himself alone. They left him to it. Yardman was riddled with so much guilt, shame, embarrassment and regret that he gave up the habit, after seeing how crack cocaine nearly made him kill his friends for a pipe.

I was surprised by the counsellor's relaxed attitudes towards us walking through Camden. It was a hazardous area, a war zone, a minefield full of shotters sniping at you from shop doorways, pubs, bus stops, kebab shops, Camden underground, Camden over-ground, outside Sainsbury's, and in the phone boxes from Camden to the West End, twenty-four seven.

I saw Lashley Judah, the person who had ran off to Colombia after buying the ocean-going yacht, leaving me to pay the bill. He'd returned to England minus the yacht, got thrown into the River Thames, survived, and ended up searching litter bins at King's Cross, Camden and the West End, head always down in search of money and crack cocaine. I felt empathy for him and told him I'd stopped using crack, and he could too. He said he was alright. I said, "But you're homeless, begging money on the streets, looking like you need a good meal, and you say you're alright?" The disease of addiction in him wouldn't budge. He was on a suicidal mission. On another occasion, I saw him by Camden Market, where he declared that I was going to be a big star one day. I thanked him with a laugh.

I'd recently written some songs at St Augustine's, including 'Love on the Internet'. That song was inspired by my acquaintance with brother G, one of the residents.

He was on the verge of tears on a daily basis, regarding a lack of communication from his girlfriend. "Go and see her, or invite her here," I said. "I can't, she lives in America," he replied. "So, where did you meet?" I asked. "On the internet," he proudly replied. I had never met someone so emotionally involved and so obsessed with someone they had never met in the flesh. I'm no stranger to fantasy but that level of obsession astonished and inspired me to write the song, 'Love on the Internet'.

Maggie was such a sensitive soul that I was afraid to touch her and watched my words very carefully when I spoke to her. She'd had a devastating childhood that'd continued into later life. She completed her treatment and less than a month later, news came to us that she'd passed away in her flat from alcoholism. Such a tender soul!

Then there was the addict who left this earth whilst leaning halfway inside a clothes bin at the top of the road, two houses away from our rehab. No doubt she was searching for clothes that she could trade for drugs. Following that, I was at an AA meeting when I heard that brother Arthur, an acquaintance from St Luke's, had relapsed and was in thrall to alcohol and cocaine, to his demise.

On my way to and from meetings, I'd pass a spiritual church. I ventured in there one day and was told that I was involved in the music business, and that I should keep at it. They said it would be rewarding.

There was an African brother who resided in the annexe to the rehab, around the corner on Agar Grove. His name was Ito and he never shared in groups. People got thrown out for that sort of thing as it's a big part of the recovery programme. St Augustine's saw fit to keep him on and helped to re-house him.

My counsellor and I got on really well. I looked forward to our one-to-ones and felt a sexual attraction between us. Her face was strained, and disappointment coloured her voice after I told her of my friendship with a tall, lovely and slender blonde lady I met at a Gospel Oak meeting of AA. She was seven years clean and sober and I thought I was with the queen of the fellowship.

We spoke regularly on the phone in the evenings and met up at meetings. We had dinner together on my birthday, at Julie's in Holland Park. I didn't listen to the rule about not getting into relationships in the first year. As soon as I was allowed a weekend away, I spent it at Maria's home. I wrote 'The Walk of Shame' on my way to a Gospel Oak meeting, on the train from Camden Road. I shared my resolve to record my songs at that meeting. Robin, a fellow member, approached me after the meeting in the car park and offered to pay for my first recording for my album 'From Rehab to Life', at a studio in Hammersmith. I was so grateful, and thanked God in my heart.

I enjoyed the session with Naz and Kiron J and stopped at Maria's place on my way back to rehab. I handed her the CD, which she played in her car CD player. She smiled and said it was a delightful sound. I told her the track was entitled 'The Walk of Shame', with more work needed to be done with it. Kiron J said it was a hit, then took the cab home. After staying a while with Maria, I caught a bus back to rehab, floating on a cloud all the way.

Maria had an eccentric mongrel dog called Benson. Eccentric because she couldn't leave him at home without coming back to a ransacked house, with urine on the carpet and sofa. She was compelled to take him everywhere with her and that included the AA meetings. Benson and I got on well. He was a rescued dog, and obviously had abandonment issues and a fear of rejection. He needed those AA meetings just like I did. There were times when I felt that Benson thought he was human.

Maria was used to going out with multimillionaires and chief executives. She gave me four years to make it in the music business or else she'd have to reconsider her position. She offered to finance my second track 'I Function'. I accepted. She was aware of my dire financial situation and supplemented whatever money I had for the recording. I was humbly grateful.

Maria was an ex-model, turned landlady. Her former husband was an ex-major, and multimillionaire West End businessman who flew his own plane that eventually took him to his own grave. She was a constantly well-groomed and high maintenance woman. I continued to progress in rehab and invited her for a meal, which we shared with some of the rehab residents. I cooked curried chicken, rice and red beans and salad. Once again, my culinary skills were hailed a success. I thanked my mother in my heart for all those cooking lessons from the age of seven.

Chapter 22

Shards of the Past:
It's a Family Affair

My life story brought up stuff about the time that I received news in prison about my son Nathan (twin to Leah) getting attacked by fifteen racially motivated youths. He was knocked unconscious and ended up in the Whittington Hospital, where he had been born. I felt so powerless, anxious and angry at not being there for him. Not sure how he was and not knowing where he lived, left me in limbo. During my stay at St Augustine's, out of the blue, I was called to the office and met by solemn faces, as I was told that the same son had been remanded in custody, in Feltham Young Offenders Institute, for grievous bodily harm (GBH).

I must go to see him I said. Miriam, my counsellor; Brendan, the head counsellor and recovering alcoholic; and John, the counsellor and recovering addict, said that I ought to not rush into it, but should put my recovery first. That infuriated me, as I told them going to see my son was part of my recovery. They said they'd have a meeting with Lana, the head principal, before they came to a decision. They were afraid that I'd relapse. I went to the Gospel Oak meeting all fired up, swearing that if those counsellors didn't allow me to visit my son, I would go anyway, even if it meant being evicted.

Imprisonment had prevented me from visiting him in hospital, but rehab wasn't going to stop me from visiting him in prison. An answer that I expected the same day, took two or three instead, during which time I was seething with rage and ready to pack up and leave, not knowing where I was going to go. My counsellor finally said, "Vander, you can go, but we'd like Peter to accompany you for your own safety." "Thank you," I replied. I resisted asking her what took them so long.

I attended my son's next court appearance at Highbury Magistrates Court. I didn't recognise him as he entered the courtroom from the dungeons below. I hadn't seen him for about four years, and his features had changed dramatically. He recognised me, and we hugged. Huge tear drops spurted from his eyes and ran down his face, as he shook with love, fear and emotion. I was humbled and thankful to God for the opportunity of being there for my son. Peter was tactful and sincere with his support. The following week, we went together to the Feltham Young Offenders Institute.

Nathan was low, with depressing stories about the prison. Suicide was a regular occurrence amongst these lost young souls. That was less heard of when I was a young offender, even though the conditions were a lot harsher then. Obviously, the answer isn't the cosmetic changes on the outside. It's about within and being able to share what or how we feel. Sharing our feelings can be the difference between life and death. I'm grateful to rehab and the fellowships for teaching me that.

Another peer, Tim, left after three months instead of six, and rented a flat next door to the rehab, with help from his rich father. With a private school education behind him, he ended up a street drunk, and wore the scars to tell the tale. All the counsellors, and some of his peers, couldn't persuade him to stay and reap the benefits of the six months course. He swore he'd be okay, with the rehab next door to remind him of the destruction of alcohol. He was determined to start a job using his father's contacts and to show him how well he could do. He felt less than a man because his father had to bail him out of bad situations and he also had to pay for rehab. That's why he didn't want to stay for the remaining three months. That decision was his downfall. Sometime later, I heard him roaring and swearing, as he swayed past our rehab like a drunken sailor.

As I lay on my single bed upstairs, with a big tree standing outside my window, and a clear blue, starless sky, studded with moving lights of aeroplanes, I listened to his voice. I felt his torment, felt his pain, and his agonised stupor. I thought he might mistake our front door for his, but he didn't. I had visited his pad once, before his relapse, but any further visits had to be put on hold, as I had to protect my recovery.

Some of us were abused by our parents, and some of us abused our parents. I empathised not only with him but also with his father, a baffled and powerless witness to his son's catalogue of drunken errors and self-destruction. He was forever trying to put humpty dumpty together again. However, the addict can only be put together again when he is willing and ready to take the right action, allowing God to do for us what no one else can.

At the Fellowships, I was busy collecting plastic chips and keyrings that marked my clean and sober sojourn. In NA, an addict with a marked desire to stop using, is given a white key ring for throwing in the towel and starting a new way of life. The addict doesn't have to be clean and sober to receive it. It was a joy, and still is, to see so many take such a courageous decision at these meetings.

The newcomer is considered to be the most important person in the room at these meetings. The older members are there to love and help the newcomer, until he or she learns to love and help themselves. It's all about progress, and not perfection in these fellowships. I endeavoured to apply that same principal in every area of my life.

As my six months in rehab approached completion, I communicated with various bodies for re-housing, with the help of Miriam, my counsellor. She was a violinist and lived with a bird, which she regularly let out of its cage. I registered with Camden Council housing and visited various housing agencies with third stage housing, geared to giving me minimal support on my way to independent housing.

I attended such an agency at Turnpike Lane. On my arrival, I scanned the walls in the waiting room, and was attracted to a music business course advert. I took down the details and started the course soon after I left rehab and moved into shared accommodation with ARP (Alcohol Recovery Project), now renamed Foundation 66, and recently amalgamated with Phoenix Futures. Without the union of these two services, Foundation 66 may not have survived much longer, due to the severe cuts in its budget. In these times of austerity, involving severe government cuts to much needed public services, I am glad that Foundation 66 united with Phoenix Futures in order to survive and continue providing a service that meets the needs of recovering addicts, alcoholics, and society as a whole.

This economic crisis was a consequence of greed, dishonesty, selfishness, and casino banking. Many bankers and others in powerful positions were acting under the influence of alcohol, heroin, cocaine, etcetera. Rehab and the two fellowships would warmly welcome them. They are a safe refuge, and ideal for the addict-alcoholic powerbroker's recovery. The fall-out from their insane actions is incalculable and ongoing. Firm closures, job losses, evictions, family fragmentation, food banks, cuts in health, education and social services to young and old alike, results in more crime and drug and alcohol addiction. No one went to jail, but at least they can go to rehab. In fact, everyone would benefit from the twelve-step programme of recovery.

These days of austerity were yet to come, as I declined to stay in a B&B even though I knew that I'd have more freedom. I also knew that I'd be more vulnerable there in Kings Cross, surrounded by the insanity of drug and alcohol abuse. Foundation 66 had a support network and a dry house policy. Although I was attracted to the freedom of the B&B, whilst waiting to be re-housed by Camden Council, I had to be honest, patient and love myself, by doing the right thing for my recovery.

Sometimes, I regretted that decision, as sharing a maisonette with two other men wasn't easy, especially when the waiting time for re-housing took much longer than the expected six to nine months. There were issues and confrontations regarding health and safety and doing a fair share of housework. I did more than my fair share, but as soon as I spoke to the other residents about it, I was accused of bullying.

I was determined to avoid another Bolingbroke. On one occasion, I approached a fellow resident about his door slamming that shook the house. His reaction was to grab me by the throat. I immediately broke his grip and tossed him on the sofa. He started to dial 999 to say that he'd been assaulted but I paid him no heed, and nothing more came of it. We were required to attend the ARP (now Phoenix Futures) drop-in centre on Pentonville Road once a week, for group therapy. I also embraced the opportunity to attend meditation classes there, run by a fellowship member called David, who had been clean and sober for many years.

I realised that I was no stranger to meditation, as I had enjoyed being still, thinking of nothing, listening to the sound of a multitude of crickets, under the light of the moon and diamond sky, as a boy in Dominica!

It was heaven! I felt connected to everything yet unattached at the same time. I began to practice meditation in my room. I was so glad to be praying again, morning and night. I have prayed all my life, and when I stopped praying during my phase of addiction, I knew something was critically wrong. I only remember praying over a pipe filled with crack cocaine, with the sole hope and wish to master the drug, instead of the drug mastering me. I would appear to be in control for a few hours, and then it was back to the paranoia. That eerie silence of the twilight zone, where I heard people in my kitchen cupboards. I stopped praying over crack after a while, as it felt like a blasphemous thing to do. After all, crack is the Devil's food. So, if you want to feed the Devil, those defects of character in you, take crack and cocaine and suffer in hell. The same applies to alcoholic drinking or the abusive use of any drug.

I thank God that I no longer have to witness crackheads searching the floor for imaginary rocks, only to find themselves smoking breadcrumbs to add to their despair. I used to pray for the wrong things, asking God to help me get away with stealing, lying, smoking crack and drinking excessively, whereas now, I pray for the strength to serve

God's will, not mine. Heaven on earth is being clean and sober, accepting life on life's terms. And the key to this is humility.

I didn't feel like I was in heaven in that little room, and I was struggling to accept my powerlessness over the people in the house and the uncertainty of when I'd be re-housed. Attending the meetings helped me remember how fortunate I was, and that a grateful heart had never relapsed.

I enrolled into the music business course at The Chocolate Factory. The tutor was Mark, an ex-pop star, and surprisingly good at his job. He was the manager of the rising star, Labrinth. We learnt about management, promotion and music production. I could've been a father to some of the students and it was good to gel with them. Mark encouraged me to record a voiceover demo, which I did, and eventually presented a forty-five-minute programme, 'On the Watchtower', for BBC1 Xtra, on the strength of it. I was earmarked to present programmes about Marcus Garvey and other great black leaders but that didn't materialise because Eddie Botsio, the programme controller, was moved to another department.

My anticipation of being a regular voice at the BBC was dashed. My disappointment at not finding regular work and income turned into gratitude for the experience. Being clean and sober opened doors to a spiritual journey within, and being a useful member of society without. Interaction, instead of isolation from society, felt good. My enthusiasm for life had returned. It was a joy, and still is, to walk the streets, free from the craving for crack and alcohol, free from the urgent and overwhelming urge to drink and drug anywhere, anytime, free from using pub lavatories, and any blind spot on the streets, or behind bushes in the park, to sneak a moment with the crack pipe.

That reminds me of the time I was to meet Nathan and Leah at Finsbury Park tube station. Nathan didn't show. I instantly used that as an excuse to spend the money I had for him on crack and booze.

Instead of saying, "Darling, give this to Nathan with love!" or offering Leah and her friend lunch or tea in a cafe, my mind was already on that train heading to Brixton, for scoring crack. That's what I did as soon as I gave her the money, with a kiss and a "Hello, how are you?" and "Goodbye!"

I had never thought that I could have been so cruel, so cold, and so selfish. Then, in the insanity of the obsession and compulsion to use, I trusted a stranger to get me some crack. He didn't deliver. In anger, I found him a little later, at a table with a well-known celebrity. The celebrity declared that he didn't know this guy, who came to sit at his table, as I demanded my money back from the stranger. Seconds later, I slapped the stranger a few times, then stopped as the celeb had female company, and the manager became alarmed with the situation.

I left, but returned to kick the fellow, and got cut on the arm with a broken glass bottle, as the stranger legged it out of there. With blood dripping, flesh dangling off my arm, I decided not to pursue him. I slotted the dangling flesh in place and secured it with my handkerchief wrapped around it and tied with a knot. Barely pausing to catch my breath, I headed for Prem's crack house in Wembley instead of going to the hospital to have the wound attended to. I only had it stitched up four days later.

With memories like that, I ought to have been the happiest man at Marquis Road in Camden Town. Instead, I fluctuated from ingratitude to gratitude, unhappiness to happiness, impatience to patience or vice versa.

At the Chocolate Factory, I co-wrote a song with Cheryl, the sister of Timothy McKenzie, the artist known as Labrinth. They had another sister there too, and they were both great vocalists. The song we co-wrote was called 'First Love'. 'First Love' was released on an album called 'Street Science', which was a collaboration between those on the course, in partnership with other up and coming talent like Sway and more established artists like Shola Ama and Gemma Fox. The album also included a different mix of my album track, 'The Walk of Shame'.

We all shared the same stage at the Karamel Club, where I performed 'The Walk of Shame'. My son Nathan attended the show, as did Maria, with Benson parked in the car outside. I was honoured by my son's presence, as the rebuilding process of our relationship had begun.

After being acquitted by Highgate Magistrates on the charge of GBH, Nathan declared himself a 'Teflon Don' on the steps outside the courthouse. I called him a joker and told him to remember the flood of tears he shed, and the fear he had concerning the conditions and suicides in HMP Feltham Young Offenders Institute, convinced that he wouldn't last long in there. It was about that time that he seriously focused on his college course, which eventually led to a university place and a degree in Business Management. Nathan and I were recovering at the same time, in different ways.

Chapter 23

Salvation Sounds

Completion of the music business course was celebrated at the expense and generosity of Mark, our tutor. Allan, a course member, became my manager. On Allan's advice, I joined Skillset, with an offer to produce and present a radio programme entitled 'Pictures of Home'.

It was a privilege to be chosen from hundreds of people to be part of the Skillset Open Door Awards Fellowship. Doors opened for me at the BBC, where I learned to produce and present radio programmes under Mary Price. She said I had a great BBC voice and asked me which station would I like my programme to go out on. I said on Radio Four. My programme would replace the much loved 'Letters from America' by Alistair Cooke. "Impossible!" Mary exclaimed. "Why?" I asked. "It just is," she replied.

I looked at that mysterious door to Radio Four, and saw myself walking through there, one day. I loved learning and working at the BBC. Allan, my manager, disappeared before he had any real input in my career as a singer-songwriter. I had no idea that he had mental health issues, which explained his sudden disappearance and lack of contact. That's the kind of behaviour that manifests itself in addiction, but he had different problems. The artist management agreement I signed with him was as thick as a book but all of a sudden, it meant nothing. Oblivious to his condition, I was angry with him at the time, as he never answered or returned my calls.

My radio programme 'Pictures of Home', featured interviews with Kathy Tyson, star of the movie 'Mona Lisa'; Claire Wright from the TV drama 'Baby Fathers'; Bunny

Stirling, first black British Commonwealth and European Boxing Champion as well as less famous members of society. All gave flashbulb memories and perceptions of where they were in their lives, seen in the context of their country of origin.

I attended Anna Scher's Drama School, where I had enrolled Leah many years before, while I was actively addicted. I was disappointed that she didn't attend the school when the time came, as she was the one who chose to go there and is a natural actress. Michelle, their mum, wasn't interested in supporting the educational and career interests of her children. Her priorities were co-dependent relationships, funding drug addicted and alcoholic boyfriends, with some emotional, mental and physical violence thrown in for good measure.

She didn't have to finance my habit, so I didn't fit in. I was shocked to discover that Michelle, the enabler, had become the user of crack, cocaine, heroin and alcohol, causing much distress to Nathan, Leah, and their older brother Anthony, who lived with them at the time. With all her faults, Michelle had a heart of gold, helped anyone in distress, and did the best that she could for her children.

On my second attendance at Anna Scher's, I was invited to a screen test for a film called 'Polly II', and played the part of Morano, the leader of modern-day pirates. He was rebelling against land grabs in an imaginary East End of London that had been suddenly submerged in water.

I took up voluntary work at the Whittington Hospital Radio Station (LNR), where I visited patients, and made sure that their requests were played. I became co-founder of a mental health charity, 'Twenty Four Eight', in Camden Town. It was later renamed 'Upbeat', as we promoted mental wellbeing through music, poetry and dance throughout London, aiming to erase the social taboo attached to mental illness. I showcased my songs at these events, held in The Irish Centre, Holiday Inn, libraries, church halls, community centres, Hackney and Islington street parties, park festivals and so on.

We started with nothing. Drew, a man from Camden Council whose name I cannot remember, and myself, with the three of us as the steering committee and subcommittee. We moved from Adelaide Road in Camden, to Holborn offices, where we had Lucia as a paid member of staff, along with sufficient space and equipment for teaching, rehearsing and recording songs, poetry and dance. We were sponsored by Cold Play, amongst others.

As the Conservatives came to power and the days of cuts and austerity began, Upbeat had to fold due to lack of local government funding and sponsorships. I'm grateful to Drew, a fellow member of the two Fellowships, for inviting me on that fulfilling journey of charity work.

I also had commitments as secretary in both fellowships and went to meetings in and out of London to book chairs (speakers) for the meetings. I was secretary at Primrose Hill, Gospel Oak, Camden Town, Hampstead, Crouch End and Marylebone meetings, on different days and times of the week, over the years. I was obliged to let go three out of the five commitments every week. I had to admit that I was people pleasing, having so much on my plate. It made me miserable with myself. I had to have balance in my life, keeping things simple and being honest with myself. These spiritual principles are as valid now as they were then, and I have maintained them to the best of my ability, a day at a time.

The estimated waiting time of six to nine months to get a flat were already over. I questioned why, when it came to my turn, things went into delayed action.

Had it anything to do with me being black? I was looking for excuses to harbour resentments, ignite anger, and excuse addiction. I had to accept life on life's terms, and understand that I was and still am, powerless over people, places and things. The only power I have is over my thoughts, words and deeds. With prayer and meditation, acts of humility, and growing acceptance of life as it is in the present moment, I kept on going.

I attended Make TV, at Islington Film School, with brother Frank. He directed, and I presented and produced a film documentary on Samuel Ajai Crowther, a slave boy who became a bishop. He's one of Frank's ancestors, and it was a privilege and pleasure to complete the project, which was premiered at the Screen on the Green in Islington and sponsored by Islington Council.

I asked Archbishop Sentamu for an interview about his views on Samuel Ajai Crowther, who was the first foreign and black Bishop of the Anglican Church. Archbishop Sentamu, of course, is a great ratifier of Samuel Ajai Crowther's legacy. The Archbishop wrote me a letter, in which he congratulated me for getting a place in Skillset and apologised for not being able to accommodate my request for an interview. I still have the letter. There I was, clean and sober, receiving a letter from the Archbishop of York.

I was going in and out of prisons, telling the truth about my experience, strength and hope in recovery. I had never foreseen that coming in a million years. I did service for the Fellowships in HMP Brixton, Wandsworth, Pentonville, Wormwood Scrubs, Feltham and Belmarsh. I also had the joy of a chance encounter with a brother at Finsbury Park who thanked me for the talk I gave in Wormwood Scrubs, because after that, he'd been attending college on release from prison and hadn't taken a drink or a drug for over one year. I thanked God for letting me know that all that service had not been in vain, as I felt the filling of the void within.

I continued to write songs anywhere, anytime, and recorded some in a cappella on a mini disc. I also attended two other film schools with Skillset. One was in Ladbroke Grove, and the other was VET Film School in Hoxton. I learned a lot about TV production at the Ladbroke Grove School and produced and presented a corporate video about the importance of time at VET. During a break outside the VET building, I sang my latest song at the time, entitled 'Love Still Remains', to a young lady office worker. "What do you think?" I asked, after one verse. She withdrew the cigarette from between her lips, gently exhaled the smoke and said, "I like it!"

I was hailed as the best student, on completion of my technical training, by VET instructor Rosalind Hewitt. I attended BBC Seminars, where I had one-to-ones with various executives at the TUC building, in Great Russell Street. I met Kristine Pommert, the senior producer of BBC World Service Religion. She was interested in my programme 'Pictures of Home'. "Some changes may be made," she said.

"I'm flexible," I replied. She gave me her card and asked me to call her. When I did, the following week, she'd already moved to another department.

I deduced that God must be telling me to focus on the music business. In so doing, I met Kiron J at Warren Street tube station, to pick up several mixes of 'Love on the Internet'. There, I inadvertently met a brother J from NA, who showed some interest in being my manager after seeing Kiron pass me the CD. We tried but it wasn't to be, for we lost contact a few months later. After recording 'The Walk of Shame' and 'I Function' in NAZ's studio in Hammersmith, I recorded two more songs, 'Every Heartbeat' and 'In Your Arms', at a studio in Colindale.

It was at that time owned by some Sony BMG employees. It was a beautiful set up in a bungalow, surrounded by spacious grounds. Inside the studio, looking out into a tree-filled garden under blue skies, felt like I was in the countryside. Kiron J said they were big songs. I agreed.

'Love on the Internet' was recorded at Michael Corby's Studio in Boston Manor. He's the son of the man who invented the Corby press, installed in millions of hotel rooms worldwide. He'd been part of the US rock band, 'The Babies'. Michael thought it was impossible to make music without drugs. He looked at me in disbelief as I said no, I had to let drugs go. He had to quit cocaine and alcohol on doctor's orders, but he seemed to be a man still in mourning for his drugs. I was honoured when Michael walked in on our session and laid some rock guitar on the track. He'd been inspired and wished me good luck with the song. I had also been inspired.

Maria, God bless her, had been helping me foot the bills. Our relationship was steady. I cooked many meals at her place and regularly walked Benson with her on Primrose Hill and Hampstead Heath, in all weathers. He had to have at least two walks a day, and it was a pleasure to interact with Maria,

Benson and nature. I looked forward to those walks as much as Benson did.

On a radiantly hot summer day, we picnicked in a grove of small trees on Primrose Hill. We had an assortment of sandwiches, cake, sparkling water, fruit juice and watermelon. Benson raced through the trees at ten miles an hour, which was all his old age would allow, but his mind said that he was doing thirty. Maria reminisced about the time when he was the fastest thing in the park. I sighed, as I watched Benson age gracefully. Humility, love, loyalty and honesty! Benson was all these things. To me, he was an example of letting go and going with the flow. Under a canopy of blue, in the heat and gentle breeze of that hazy and glorious day, time stood still, as I experienced heaven on earth. Maria, Benson and I, were enveloped in an eternal moment of bliss.

In reality, her warning of four years without success and she'd be off, played on my mind. Two years later, I was still in temporary housing. Offers of making quick and substantial sums of money came my way, but I said no. I was committed to a more spiritual life in the slow lane. With no flat in sight and a music-deal some way off, I was surviving on benefits. Nonetheless, I accepted my situation.

Acceptance gave me back my power and helped free me from the painful uncertainties in life, love, and finance. I kept writing songs and kept an open mind about where I'd live.

Maria decided to move into one of her properties in Southend, while letting out her Hampstead home in London. Before doing so, she left me some household goods and furniture in storage. Her friend Debbie, who was moving to the States, also made a kind contribution, for which I remain grateful. They were the queens of the fellowship. John Edwards, whom I met at a Hampstead meeting, became my sponsor. He was a successful artist, and basically helped me through steps four to twelve.

Step four involves making a searching and fearless moral inventory of ourselves, and step five is about revealing to God and man the exact nature of our wrongs. These steps helped me walk through the arch of freedom, feeling lighter and more comfortable in myself. Under the regime, I got to know and understand the nature of my addiction, which is full of ego, full of fear, rife with defects of character and shortcomings. It was more than a confession. It was cleaning house to let God in. I got to know my assets alongside my catalogue of personal weaknesses.

I felt a presence in John's art studio, with extra light streaming through the skylight, while John sat motionless, as if in a trance, as I read what I had written for step four. It took me two working days to read it all. My assets came up as love, loyalty, creativity, helping others, and a willingness to do the right thing, while my faults were legion. I thank God that today I realise the limitations of ego. Peace of mind is everything. After a losing battle with cancer, John is no longer with us, and I'm grateful to him for his time, patience and advice. He said that I was more spiritual than him but was helpful in advising me on practical matters of the day. Thank you, John!

Benson passed away at the animal hospital in Finsbury Park. He simply slumped on his legs and never recovered. I still remember Maria comforting him as he shook uncontrollably, peeing on the floor, as tears ran down her cheeks.

So, Maria moved to Southend, and I moved to Crouch Hill. I admired how she had faithfully attended to her husband Gerald, an ex-army major and businessman, who'd suffered brain damage after being hit by his aeroplane propeller. Those weekly hospital visits lasted seventeen years. After several visits to her bungalow by the sea, our relationship faded. We lasted four years, and she'd been true to her word, as I looked towards establishing myself in the music business.

Chapter 24

Of Death, Home and Healing, and the High Court

The flat that I moved into, was small and only around the corner from Nathan, Leah and their mother, who lived in a house on Crouch Hill. I witnessed their pain as they watched their mother slowly committing suicide with crack cocaine, heroin, alcohol and pills. Then, there was the shame of seeing her on the Elthorne Park bench around the corner, with other alcoholics and drug addicts. I told them she suffered from the insanity of addiction, which involves denial, dishonesty and selfishness. "I've been there myself!" I exclaimed. But it did little to ease Leah's fears, or Nathan's anger towards their mother.

I seized the opportunity to make amends with Nathan, Leah and their mum, in any way I could, by asking for forgiveness for abandoning them in the past. I also asked them in what way could I be of any help in the present moment.

Michelle just wanted me to tell Nathan to leave her alone or move out. I asked her to consider rehab. I put a book of where to find all the meetings through her letterbox, but she wasn't ready. She had counselling certificates, and had worked in recovery professionally, allocating rooms and flats to addicts and alcoholics. It was a confusing and devastating situation. It got to the point where I'd hide from her, in order to avoid the shame I felt every time she introduced me as her ex-husband to her group of friends on the park bench.

Seeing her, and her friends in that state, helped me to be grateful for being clean and sober. This brought recollections of when I sought custody of Nathan and Leah, through the

Royal Courts of Justice. Their mother had sold the house behind my back, kept all the money, and swanned off to Antigua with her boyfriend called Nuts, another alcoholic addict. Nathan and Leah were left without secure accommodation, and with no knowledge of when their mother would return. They were moving from one house to another, sometimes sleeping on the floor or flea-ridden mattresses. All too often, I had to turn detective in order to find their whereabouts.

I was living in Putney, southwest London, while they were miles away, across the river in North London. I was reluctant to move them from their primary school and friends in Crouch End but felt compelled to do so in the circumstances. I also thought that once they were under my care, I'd find the strength to kick the habit.

Michelle failed to appear at the court hearings twice. The judge then ordered that she be apprehended and brought to court. The airports were also alerted to look out for her. After many months, we had no idea as to whether she was in or out of the country. But one lead suggested that she'd returned.

She appeared at the next hearing looking forlorn, confused and out of it, no longer the dapper lady that I once knew. She asked me for money, saying that she'd left her purse in a phone box. It reminded me of the lies I'd told in order to get money for crack, cocaine and alcohol. As a result, I refused to give or lend her any money. She'd reputedly bought a property in Antigua. What happened to the rest of the money? I didn't ask her. She'd sold the house for three hundred and fifty thousand pounds, when it was worth over five hundred thousand pounds at the time.

In disbelief, she asked me why was I seeking custody, apparently unaware of the stress, strain and instability she'd heaped on Nathan, Leah and Anthony, who were still living at home. I told her that I thought she'd be happy to continue along the road that she was travelling, while I took custody of the twins. Things were in a terrible mess, and Nathan and Leah were the innocent victims. I myself must admit that I always attended the High Court with lots of alcohol, and crack cocaine in my system. I became anxious and fearful about my ability to properly care for Nathan and Leah but was doggedly determined to do so. I bought a bunk bed for them from Mamie's catalogue. Mamie paid for it, as I failed to keep up with the payments.

Once reunited with their mother, I asked Nathan and Leah who would they prefer to live with, mummy or daddy? I was convinced that they'd choose me. At the tender age of nine, both of them looked at me sheepishly, then at each other, then looked at me again, and simultaneously said "mummy". I was gutted by their response. The void within deepened and expanded immeasurably, with the pain that came from their answer.

I began to resent them and their decision, but eventually let it go, as I, suicidally, resorted to more drug and alcohol abuse. Consequently, I dropped my case for custody at the next hearing. The bunk bed was sold in order to buy more crack. There was no way I would fight for custody against their wishes.

I was living in my own space, above a brother who'd moved in the flat underneath. He was a DJ by the name of Matt. A shy and quiet soul, he was in a relationship with Sharon, who self-harmed, and was pregnant. They argued continually, as their relationship hung on a thread. I empathised with the situation, but not when their marathon arguments kept me awake till after three or four a.m.

My new home was only a stone's throw away from the Whittington Hospital, where I worked on the radio station. It was at the bus stop outside the hospital on Highgate Hill, where I met Muriam. She introduced me to Phil Harris, founder member of the band 'Ace', who had the worldwide number one hit with, 'How Long Has This Been Going On'. She gave me his phone number, and said she'd let him know that I'd be in touch.

I felt as if life was saying that I belonged in the music-business, and to keep going, regardless of appearances. I became friends with Simon, Jules, Harpic and with everyone I met at Radio LNR (London Network Radio). Simon, an ex-Choice FM DJ, and Harpic, an ex-minder to Marvin Gaye, helped me in the production of my radio programme, 'Pictures of Home', and with my voice show reel. Jules, a singer-songwriter, helped to set me up on Myspace. I'm thankful to them and other members of staff, including security, who worked at the radio station. Unfortunately, government cuts and hospital politics resulted in the closure of the station, which was a great shame, since Hospital Radio LNR did a lot of charitable work, and raised a lot of money for good causes, long before I came along.

Having dumped all the rubbish that had kept me sick from childhood, by steps four and five, I was travelling a lot lighter. I now had love and forgiveness for myself and for others and began to feel free from negative emotions and a troubled past. I began to understand the nature of addiction and ego, in a myriad of salient and subliminal forms. It's the illness that convinces me that I'm well when I'm not. The ego, telling me that it's impossible to have defects of character and shortcomings removed. In a nutshell, the ego demands edging God out.

However, God is the only power through whom, with whom, and by whom, the ego, the source of all my fears, and my addiction, is uprooted. Having relied on the ego for so long, I had to be ready to go through the painful and gradual process of letting it go, as God will not remove the defects of character and shortcomings without my willingness.

Steps six and seven are known as the forgotten steps in both fellowships, because people generally believe that the ego is a useful tool for protection, and for getting them what they want. All the same, I was shocked by the lack of support in both fellowships when I shared my confidence in God removing defects of character and shortcomings, just as he had removed my obsession and compulsion to use. Thinking that it's impossible to survive without ego in this world, where all is vanity, was no longer part of my mind-set. Instead of forgetting, I chose to remember these steps every day and not deny but relinquish the worship of vanity.

I grew in awareness of the fact that the ego was an obstacle to the true fulfilment of my purpose on earth. The ego was a useless tool (look at where it had gotten me), a figment of my imagination, and an obstacle to true love, peace and happiness.

I felt that the fear of going through the pain of its extraction was worth it. Thus, I humbly asked God to remove all the defects of my character. The process is ongoing, and now I am appreciating the benefits of less stress and strain, emotional balance, and more peace of mind, in all areas of my life.

In step seven, I asked God, the creator, to remove all my shortcomings. Shortcomings included falling short, being economical with the truth, quick-tempered, self-justifying, and quick to judge others, instead of taking stock of myself. Yes, I felt that these shortcomings were a stumbling block to happiness and peace of mind. God had removed my obsession and compulsion to use drugs and alcohol. After receiving such a miraculous demonstration, I trusted that God would free me from all my defects of character and shortcomings, as long as I remained humbled and entirely ready to let them go. Otherwise, they weren't going anywhere. This was a slow process, and I had to be patient and vigilant in thought, word and deed.

I went into step eight and made a list of people I'd harmed and became willing to make amends to them all. I made amends to family, friends and others that I managed to locate, or suddenly met by chance. I wrote letters to those I couldn't locate. The souls departed, and the rest were left to be dealt with in God's time, not mine. I was making amends to God and to myself in the process, and this is ongoing. It was all about clearing the wreckage of the past. It didn't matter whether the person did me wrong or vice versa. It didn't matter if they refused to forgive me. All that mattered was that I do my best, ask God to forgive me, forgive myself and keep my side of the street clean.

It was a humbling and healing experience, as I saw people's faces come alight, with most of them congratulating me on my recovery. They said they didn't want anything more than to see me clean and sober, living a better way of life.

There were injured parties that my sponsor advised me not to chance meeting, as it might lead to war, imprisonment, hospital or the morgue.

I felt that I'd freed others and myself from the pain of the past, allowing us to grow spiritually. This growth was instant. I saw it and felt it in others as well as in myself, on every occasion that I expressed step nine, which required that I 'make direct amends to such people wherever possible, except when to do so would cause injury.' My daughter Naomi sent me a text the moment I thought about her. It read, "I forgive you." I thought she'd forgiven me years ago, but obviously not. The process is gradual and slow. Delighted to receive that message, I thanked her, and asked if there was anything I could do for her. Be there for her and her siblings whenever they need me, came the reply. "I will, by the grace of God," I said. The days of instant gratification and quick fixes were over.

Chapter 25

What's New? The Awakening

In step ten, I continue to take personal inventory, and when I'm wrong, I promptly admit it. I continue to practice that step every day. As a result, I keep the temple clean, rather than leaving an accumulation of defects and shortcomings to fester. Thus, I maintain peace of mind, emotional balance, and a solid defence against drink and drugs. So doing, I create the right conditions for letting God in, and ego out. In recovery, this is called a Maintenance Step.

I practice step eleven every day, which is, 'seeking through prayer and meditation, to improve our conscious contact with God as we understand him, praying only for knowledge of his will for us, and the power to carry it out.' Prayer and meditation over nine years have brought me to a level that naturally lets God in and ego out. Now, I have the ability to be calm and assertive. Now, I have long fuses instead of short ones. Prayer and meditation slows, stills and empties my mind of all the rubbish that's adverse to my recovery. So, I'm like a tree planted by a river, bearing fruit in due season.

Step twelve says, 'Having had a spiritual awakening as a result of these steps, we carry this message to alcoholics, and drug addicts, practicing these principals in all our affairs.' This is a gradual process, and now, at last, with constant practice of the twelve steps, I am spiritually awake, carrying the message to the suffering addict and alcoholic, through love, service, meditation and prayer.

Living in the light of all twelve steps, and expressing spiritual principles in all my affairs, attracts others to follow suit. This service, prayer and meditation began with the fellowships, and helped me to become a productive member of society, living a life that's useful and whole. This is my experience after constantly practicing all the steps, as required, on a daily basis. The fellowships say steps six and seven are the forgotten steps. And like I said earlier, I make sure I remember them every day, for they deal with the illness that kept me enslaved. The twelve steps haven't erased all the trials and tribulations of life but have given me the strength to face difficulties and avoid many pitfalls.

The serenity prayer, 'God grant me the serenity, to accept the things I cannot change, courage to change the things I can, and wisdom to know the difference,' is the main prayer of the fellowships. Armed with this, anytime, anywhere, I have reserves of strength. There have been times when I've recited the prayer constantly, just to get me through the day, keeping negative thoughts at bay. Now, I have the wisdom to know what I can and cannot change.

And then it happened, that one day I rose at dawn, and was about to pray and meditate, when I heard the voice of an angel singing, 'What's So New'. Gratefully, I wrote the first line and then spontaneously wrote the rest of the verse. Thanking God, I left it at that.

Determined to complete my album, I phoned Phil Harris. He was friendly on the phone, and like a brother when we met for the first time, at his house in Muswell Hill. He was a very upbeat individual. Immediately, I felt at home, and sang him songs, while he made tea. After a line or two, he'd say sing something else.

After several songs, I decided to sing 'What's So New'. Before I could complete the first line, he decided that was the song he'd like to create with me. I explained that I only had one verse and agreed to come back after I completed the song. When I returned with the finished article, Phil asked about the intention behind the song. "To help me get through the door of the music business," I replied. Phil voiced his approval by saying that this song will definitely get me through the door. I accepted his words as a prophecy waiting to be fulfilled. I agreed with him that more work needed to be done on the tracks I'd previously recorded. So, with a cup of tea, biscuits, acoustic guitar and vocals, Phil and I began to lay out the blueprint for 'What's So New'? I sang while Phil played, and in this age of hi-tech, our first demo of the song was recorded on cassette!

I enjoyed constructing and shaping the song with this great guitarist, and looked forward to our sessions in his home, at his convenience. Phil revealed to me that he had medical complications with his heart and other issues. So, we'd spend two to three hours a time on the song, in between trips to hospital, his doctor and his daughters. He said he was working with me for love, and not for money. I deeply appreciated Phil's help and making his acquaintance, and I still do.

Phil had turned his back on Hollywood and returned to a simple life in Muswell Hill. He turned down hugely lucrative work, before and during the time we worked together. I'd turn up at his flat with mangoes and other fruits, or a bottle of cognac for his table. That was Phil's only vice. A bottle of cognac would last him about two months. I was also surprised to know that he had his face and chin rebuilt, after an accident in a Ferrari on a mountain road in Southern France. Somehow, these revelations opened a window on a world I had never associated him with. A world of brotherly love.

On the surface, you'd never think Phil was ill. We recorded 'What's So New?' within a year, at Palace Studios, with a lot of help from Micky Portman. He was nominee for best soundtrack at an Edinburgh film festival. Anyone who listens to TV would've heard some of his backing tracks to various programmes. Phil and I agreed to make more songs together.

Unfortunately, he became less and less available as his health deteriorated. I thought he'd been avoiding me, but that wasn't the case, as Micky revealed Phil's passing after a major surgery. More than ever, it seemed a privilege to have known him. Thank you, Phil and Micky. I also thank the band Ace, for the joy and inspiration I receive every time I hear your classic number one song, 'How Long Has This Been Going On'.

As I sit here with pen in hand, I remember that the Christmas before I came into recovery was spent in a crack house. The place was eerie, void and depressing. My mind was far from family, as I wondered where my next pipe was coming from. Parma looked at me from the dingy hallway outside the room where I sat and exclaimed, "You're a messenger, so go and give the message!" "I will," I replied. That message was God's gift to me that Christmas.

Again, there was another brother on the top deck, at the back of a bus, who said to me with authority, "You must return to the music business. A big fortune awaits you there. The greatest pain is failing to fulfil our purpose on this earth." I knew exactly what he meant. It felt like it was another communication from God.

Stunned, I blurted out, "Are you Archangel Michael, come to deliver a message?" "I don't know if I'll ever see you again," was his distant response, "but the reason why I'm on this bus is to give you that message." The moment before he spoke, I'd been singing reggae and soul songs, as if I was performing to an audience. God's message was loud and clear, and the suffering I had endured in order for his message to get through, had been worth it.

So, there I was, on track, in my little flat, although in financial and emotional pain, from lack of money, and a lady in my life. I was fairly resolved to staying away from criminality, even if it offered a fast track to financial fortune. I had to remember that I'd tried that route time and time again, and where had it gotten me? On my travels, a shady character offered me a way to make a quick seventy thousands pounds or more. I was really tempted, so I talked to a member of the fellowship about it, at his home in Belsize Park. He said I had free will, but to remember that dishonesty would consign me to hell.

I was missing the comforts of having a car, paying my bills and shopping for food, clothes and drink without worrying about the cost. I missed owning the best sound equipment, booking a recording studio for as long as I needed it, giving my children what they wanted, and taking tropical holidays. Yes, I missed all that, but I said no to easy money. I was offered a cool one hundred thousand pounds on another occasion and turned it down. I walked into a restaurant and was offered a kilo of coke and turned it down. I was offered many kilos of cocaine, and I still turned them down.

Yet when I asked for loans to help me record my songs, people all over London turned me down. Strange that some were willing to trust me with a hundred thousand pounds worth of cocaine rather than invest five thousand pounds in honest work I needed to do. On benefits, and desperate to fulfil my purpose as a singer-songwriter, I started part-time work as a chef. My sister Verina, and her lifetime partner, John, bought me the chef's knives and uniform I needed, to get me started with an agency.

Around that time, I got a part in a movie entitled 'Last Move', playing a gangster boss. It gave me the opportunity to reflect on where I was, and where I am today. That movie took about two years to complete, and during that time, I worked at many locations as a chef. My favourite ones were the concerts at Wembley Stadium with U2, Jay Z and Coldplay amongst others. I sang in the kitchens and gave away demo CDs of my songs. I made sure that they all knew that I was in transition from part-time chef to professional singer-songwriter. My colleagues in the catering division were very supportive and even bought copies of my demos.

During that time, I attended a Madonna Hard Candy concert at Wembley Stadium with my nephew, James. I felt connected to her. It was a great show! I looked at the director's boxes and wondered how the chefs were doing. It felt good to be at Wembley as a spectator. "Even better when I'm here performing," I thought. My connection with Madonna and her performance was enhanced by the spiritual messages on the stage screen.

I thought of all the suffering alcoholics I'd spotted amongst the chefs. So, I used to say, that I had a huge drink and drug problem, until I went into rehab and joined the fellowships. Planting a seed and trusting that it will grow by the grace of God, clearly had results. I don't intend to glorify drinking and drugging, violence and immorality. All these things end in jails, mental institutions, death and destruction.

Having been so far down a road on which so many have perished, it would be immoral and vile to make that world attractive to others. It's not part of the recovery process, and not something I wish on family, friends or enemies. Undeniably, some books, films, and music helped to propel me down a negative path. At the same time, the music business is often in bed with the underworld, and many artists rise to prominence with dubious backing. Banks fight shy of supporting artistic endeavours, and since their fall from grace, have become even more entrenched.

The recent passing of Pepe, a flamboyant Rastaman, opened a floodgate of memories of 64 Rushmore Road, Clapton E5, where a huge amount of music and ganja business transactions were energised by the stream of people who frequented and stayed in that house. The crowd included the likes of Bob Marley and the Wailers, Tappa Zukie, Bunny Lee, and many more, including me. Pepe got Trevor Walters high in the charts with a version of Lionel Ritchie's songs 'Stuck on You' and 'Easy'. Those were the days of prosperity! And liked or disliked, Pepe was an influential figure.

All of which brings memories of Asher and his house in Median Road, around the corner from Hackney Police Station, with a record shop below that was run by Pepe. The rest of his house ran along similar lines to Pepe's. Cooking and eating was always central to these houses, as was the case at mine, and I always contributed to the pot in some way. Asher told those who frequented his house, about his trips to see me perform as lead singer of the Trax at Saint Jude's Church Hall, in Blurton Road E5, and Cardinal Pole School assembly hall. Asher would 'big me up' in that way, and as certain eyes looked at me in surprise, I was humbled and grateful for the encouragement.

And that reminds me of Rodi, with whom I worked producing Sugar Minnot, Trevor Hartley and the Heptones. Like Asher, he left London and went to New York, where I heard that he got rich quick. I'd like to thank him in his absence, for his help and encouragement, on my journey in the music business.

So many people I knew had been killed in America that I wouldn't go, not even when tickets were bought, and a man sent to my home to accompany me on the trip. It seemed as if life had little value over there.

Lacey, the brother who'd sent for me, never got to move into the mansion he bought on Long Island, as he was fatally shot by police. Those were the days of prosperity, and to be struggling later on in life, when I ought to be taking it easy, came as a shock at first. Then it became a blessing and not a curse, as I realised that I have the health, strength, enthusiasm and talent to help others through my experiences. As I was on benefits, I understood I could only work sixteen hours a week, so that's what I did, in my desperation to complete my album.

What began at a cost of two and a half thousand pounds, turned into five thousand pounds, then seven thousand four hundred pounds, and finally thirteen thousand four hundred pounds. The couple I only refer to as P and K, knew my position and said they'd like to help me, but apparently, they were only out to help themselves.

In those circumstances, I increased my hours of work as a chef and even faked time sheets. In fact, the cost far exceeded thirteen thousand four hundred pounds and I spent so much on faulty equipment from them that wouldn't even get five pounds at cash converters. I spent more money on printing that was substandard and paid them for photos which I never received. I even bought ink cartridges for their printer and ended up paying more for the low-quality printing than others did for better quality production from them. Dealing with these people was a very painful and frustrating experience, yet I'm grateful for their service, and for an experience which I wouldn't wish on anyone.

I knew I was taking a risk exceeding sixteen hours on occasion, but deemed the risk was worth it. The thought of imprisonment didn't deter me from taking that risk.

I must say I enjoyed working at Royal Ascot in the Royal enclosure, in the Champagne Lounge, where I served finely decorated lobsters, crabs and other seafood. I enjoyed the sight of the most beautiful women in haute couture, especially on Ladies Day. It was a scene I was glad to be part of, as a humble chef. I played 'What's So New' on a portable CD player, as other chefs gathered round to listen. They liked the song and wished me well with my music career. I cherish my memories of Ascot and would love to sing there one day.

Occasionally, I did some decorating, and found myself playing 'Love on the Internet'. Everybody sat still, looked at me and insinuated that I was wasting my talent painting and decorating. I didn't tell them that the money from the job was paying for my album tracks, but simply thanked (God) them for their approval. At the time, I was struggling to keep my phone on, and pay my bills. Gas, electricity and water payments were always in arrears, while my larder ran out of the quality food I was used to.

After the death of my relationship with Maria, years went by without girlfriends or sex, as I channelled my energy into prayer, meditation, music, exercise and fellowship meetings. I enjoyed jogging in Highgate Woods, sitting under a tree in prayer and meditation, exercising at home and in the gym. Disciplining myself in this way, practicing Tai Chi, I became content to let events unfold naturally. From somewhere, the next lady in my life was surely moving my way.

At one point, a whole studio was moved into my home to voice some tracks, and it was then that I had the pleasure of recording 'Love Conquerors Hate' with my son, Troopz, and 'When I Was With You' with Apollo and 'Love Still Remains' with Indeed I. I ended paying an exorbitant price, even though the equipment was in my home, with me footing the electricity bill as well. Doing this, I learnt the meaning of sacrifice.

Chapter 26
Unconditional Love

Anytime I visit my sister Verina's home, she always fills a couple of bags with groceries for me to take away, without me having to ask. My stepfather, Clive, has given me money from time to time without my asking, and even when I've felt compelled to say something. Meeting with unconditional love has helped me grow spiritually, mentally and emotionally.

During recovery, I've seen my mother's health deteriorate from walking and talking to being speechless, bedbound, and being fed food and medication intravenously. Observing her suffering with Alzheimer's, angina, high blood pressure and an infection eating away a hole in her flesh, the consultant gave her a few weeks to live.

Clive decided the best thing he could do in the circumstances was to take her home. He prepared a room for her where she could receive medication and water intravenously. As a result, she has made so much progress that she can eat pureed meals, with a little milk, yoghurt and fruit juice. Even her bedsores and a raft of infections have disappeared. Mum has made a miraculous recovery, through the power of love, medication and Moringa. I visit her every week, and speak to her as I normally would, telling her what's happening in my life, and the grandchildren's and so on.

My brother, Glen, is suffering from MS (Multiple Sclerosis) and recovering from prostate cancer in Florida, and has a lovely, loving wife, a son Glen Junior and a beautiful elder daughter, Rashida, now married. His first son, Curtis, who is back in London, worked as a policeman and currently as a counsellor. Can you believe it? My sister Verina is suffering from arthritis so badly in her knees, hands and back that it's a miracle how she still works at a primary school and conducts dance lessons elsewhere. It is with deep sadness that I'm compelled to say that our beloved and beautiful sister Verina left this world on the 28th of August 2018 after suffering many years of chronic pain from arthritis and sarcoidosis of the lungs which severely diminished her ability to breathe. I sang *What's become of the broken hearted* (by Jimmy Ruffin) at her funeral, hoping that she's found love, peace and happiness on the other side of life and with immeasurable gratitude for her support that encouraged and helped me to create and finance my album 'Every Heartbeat' which I renamed 'From Rehab to Life' many years later.

There's angry Nathan, whom I kept visiting at the house he shared with his mother. While she was in active addiction, he was in despair, bewildered by her selfish destructive behaviour. It's difficult for most people to understand that addiction is a spiritual, mental and physical illness where the will, instead of saying no, bows down in thrall to drugs and alcohol.

There's Leah, in a turbulent relationship with the father of her two sons, Jayson and Israel. I have repeatedly told her that it's best not to rely on any man. I'm glad to say that she's started a teacher's training course and is now attending university.

Furthermore, my twin daughters Naomi and Makeda, and their brothers Immanuel and Nathaniel, hardly speak to me, since I had a disagreement with their mother Rhoda. She had asked me to lie on Nathaniel's behalf, in order to fast track him out of a mental institution in Edinburgh, Scotland, after getting into trouble with the police. The details of the altercation were very vague.

In the knowledge that he had lied, controlled and manipulated Rhoda from a child, I said that the only way he was going to recover was with the truth. Even if it meant that his move would be delayed, God would be with us. Furthermore, I phoned Nathaniel and his psychiatrist on separate occasions, telling the latter that he could use my address for Nathaniel's referral to London. But I wasn't going to say that he'd be living with me, and I would only go along if it was an absolute requirement. There'd be no drinking and drugging in my flat!

I now know that the truth sets us free from anything, and mental illness is no exception. As Nathaniel was a compulsive liar, he needed the example of truth, and without it his recovery would be a figment of the imagination. He got to London soon enough, on the strength of my address alone, and was quickly re-housed, which wouldn't have happened otherwise. But the rift caused, by my not siding with her totally, is still there and has influenced his brother, Immanuel and his twin sisters, Naiomi and Makeda, in being distant from me to this day, just when I thought our relationship was on the mend.

There's my sister Sandra, very overweight, with other health issues. She needs to get out and be more active. My youngest sister, Antigua, has Down's Syndrome, and lives in a lovely supported home. She has above average intelligence for her condition, and reads, writes, and enjoys regular trips abroad. She can't handle mum's present condition and became reluctant to visit her regularly. She loves listening to music and retreating into doing her own thing.

And there's Daddy Clive, who had a triple heart bypass operation recently. His recovery is up and down, and needs to stabilise. His greatest anxiety and concern is for mum's welfare, in case he dies before she does.

Most recently, my sister Heather suffered a stroke. I understand it to be the result of decades spent pleasing others instead of pleasing herself, while she kept her pain and disappointments inside. Together with my own personal struggles, much of this provided triggers for using but not anymore, by the grace of God, the fellowships and the twelve steps.

Rehab, and all these drug and alcohol agencies play vital roles in the recovery process. I go on about it because in order to maintain lifelong recovery on a daily basis, God, the fellowships and the twelve steps are the solution. Without God and the twelve steps of recovery, I wouldn't be where I am today.

Twenty-ten saw me performing live shows with bands at Leyton Football Ground, the Ship Aground on Lea Bridge Road, a big club in Sheffield-, and Picketts Lock in Liverpool, twice, with the Earth Defender reggae label run by Ras Howard. I shared the same stage with Don King Pin, Rowan Irie, Headless, Mystic Messenger, Ghostman, Ras Howard, Eugene Paul, Christine Joywhite, Sister Andake, Foley Don, Mental Illness, Riki Tiki, Ras Kinah, Singing Hanna, Cornbread, and Errol Dunkley. Rehearsing and travelling around the country with these artists in a battered van, with a Dominican Rastaman as a conscious driver, was an unforgettable and enjoyable experience.

Russell Vander Puye, director of Atori Films, also invited me to play a bigger role as a gangster boss in a film, originally called 'Sticks and Stones', but later changed to 'Buzzing' for legal reasons. It's the follow up to 'Last Move'. Its release has been cancelled on several occasions, and it's still unclear when it will be premiered. I got involved in those movies because they didn't glorify gangs, drugs, and violence, but made one reconsider going down that road or turning off it, as the case may be.

A month after I left the chef world, I received a letter from the Department of Works and Pensions (DWP), asking me to attend a meeting at their office in Marylebone to answer questions regarding working whilst on benefits. This came as no surprise. The thought of losing income support and housing benefit weighed heavily on my mind, but gradually eased as I accepted the situation for which I was responsible. I attended my appointment and brought a hard copy of my album along, which still needed mixing and mastering, despite the money spent on it, although I had already paid for that to be done.

After shaking hands and introducing himself, Peter, from the DWP, produced a record of payments I'd received for chef work, and for appearing in the Muller yoghurt advertisement. It was a large piece of paper, and the list was long.

I was disgusted to find that I was a victim of false accounting, as the records showed me earning forty pounds an hour in some cases. Inflating the total, they said I owed almost ten thousand pounds. The most I'd ever earned was ten pounds an hour. I asked him to chase the agency, as these figures were incorrect. I figured the most I owed to be about two and a half thousand pounds. I didn't work every day, every week, or every month. It was staggering to see how my dishonesty uncovered the dishonesty of the agency I'd worked for.

Peter was reluctant to question the agency's figures. As to why I did it, I simply presented my album and said, "This is why." Furthermore, I said the lack of financial support from family and friends left me no option, as I felt it was my destiny to complete that album. It dawned on me that I could've avoided that situation, had I informed them of my part-time work. We shook hands again as he said he'd let me know of his decision by letter. As expected, I was charged with owing the DWP ten thousand pounds and was summoned to appear at Horseferry Road Magistrates for fraud. Though not guilty of that amount, and with the cuts in funding legal-aid, I pleaded guilty and was spared a jail sentence, and tagged instead. That meant I had to be indoors from nine p.m. until seven a.m. the next day, for two months. Furthermore, I was given a three months prison sentence, suspended for one year. I left the courthouse and walked to Victoria Station, in a grey suit in the rain, glad the case was over, though not yet closed.

Chapter 27

Of Death, Home and Healing, Part II

The tag had long gone, when I received a phone call from Leah one Sunday morning, anxiously asking me to go to Nathan. "He's crying over mum's body on the bedroom floor, unable to wake her," she continued. I knew their mother had left us at that moment. By the time I arrived, Leah was already there with Nathan weeping, as they gently, and lovingly, stroked their mother's body.

By painful degrees they realised that their mother wasn't going to sit up or say a word in that body ever again. The corpse's face had partially turned purple, with tracks of blood from her nostrils. An old mink coat was on the big brass bed I bought a long time ago. There was dog poo on the floor. The mink and diamond lady passed away in squalor. Deep down, we knew this was a consequence of drug and alcohol addiction.

We were joined by Simone, their elder sister, as the police arrived. Anthony, an older brother, turned up later. I comforted them all, the best I could in the situation, while my eyes watered without a tear. Nathan appeared to be the most distraught, riddled with anger, guilt, regret, shame and remorse at having lost the opportunity to make peace with his mum. They had only just spoken of reconciliation, after identifying their grandma Lila's body, Michelle's mum, in the morgue at the Royal London Hospital in Whitechapel, the day before. For their mother to leave so suddenly, less than a day later, was a double tragedy.

This situation reminded me that I'm powerless over life on life's terms. I could only help everyone accept the situation. Their mother's body was in the morgue for six weeks, while they set about finding money and making funeral arrangements. Leah ensured that her mother's corpse was transported by horse and carriage, while the father of her sons helped as best as he could towards that aim. Grief had a way of bringing people together, just like addiction does in rehabs and in the fellowships. I clearly remember the clattering of horse's hooves coming to a halt, outside the house on Crouch Hill. We left the building to attend the funeral service with family members from Manchester that none of us had met before. Our former neighbour, Claire, also a Mancunian, was a tower of strength in helping them through their bereavement.

The grieving continues even now, with Nathan receiving counselling, while Leah had a second son, Israel. Anthony is getting on with his life with a lady, after being celibate for many years. Simone is soldiering on, minus her youngest son, who has ended up in care. Their brother and Simone's twin, Jayson, has been sectioned under the Mental Health Act and is still unable to connect with his mother's passing, because of constant medication as well as drug addiction.

I attend my grandson, Jayson's school whenever I'm invited to various events. He is Leah's first son. We went on a school trip to the Royal Festival Hall, where I helped to shepherd some of the children with other parents and teachers. The London Philharmonic, conducted by a name I do not recall, performed classical music to accompany a selection of children's stories. The acoustics were brilliant! You could hear a pin drop from a distance. My desire for performing at the venue grew by the minute. To hear an audience of innocent youngsters, full of zest for life, singing along to classical music, as the lyrics appeared on a silver screen above the orchestra, was heaven on earth.

We lunched with children from other schools on the grass on the South Bank of the Thames, under the watchful London Eye. I greeted a man from the fellowship for alcoholics based in Primrose Hill. He was distributing black bin bags for the rubbish, and clearly enjoying being a useful member of society. I watched the children with a fatherly eye, as they played with screams of laughter on that sun-drenched, hilly lawn.

I wondered what path they'd take in life. No one in their right mind would introduce or expose children to drugs and alcoholic drinking. What a joy to be free from that insanity and irresponsibility.

My grandson Jayson held my hand constantly, all the way to the venue, and back to school. It was his way of saying, "This is my granddad!" Some of the boys' backpacks were almost as big as them, prompting me to offer my services as bagboy. Next thing I knew, I was carrying four or five bags.

The whole experience was exhilarating as well as exhausting, and one I'd gladly repeat, should the opportunity arise again. To be a mother or father is life's greatest honour, privilege, and pleasure, and having abused that duty in the past, it's a mercy to be making amends, by the grace of God.

Chapter 28

Skin I'm in, the Musical
Road from Rehab to Life

After all these years, still in the red, still economically insecure, without a girlfriend and growing older, I suddenly found myself in a fearless place. Through constant prayer, meditation, love and forgiveness of past and present, by serving others within and without the fellowships, carrying the message of recovery, and practicing spiritual principles in all my affairs, on a daily basis, I attained peace of mind.

I began to experience freedom from fear of people, places and things, freedom from financial insecurity, and freedom from loneliness. I found myself resolving situations that used to baffle me. I began to act on intuition. I embraced my feelings and became unafraid to express them. Liberated from defects of character, I no longer felt the need, urge or desire to act them out. Being relaxed and comfortable in my own skin felt so good. The Higher Power that freed me from the bondage of alcoholism and drug addiction had, after so many years, freed me from the bondage of ego.

Suddenly, I realised that I didn't have to be a multibillionaire and a great success in the music business to feel safe, secure, and strong within. It was a revelation! In my days of financial prosperity, I never felt true happiness. I had never believed that one could be happy without material wealth, but constant practice of the twelve steps proved otherwise. I do not reject material success, I'm simply saying it's good to feel comfortable in my skin, with or without it. Being that way hasn't dampened my enthusiasm and desire for success, but simply strengthened my patience and confidence that success is imminent. God has given me a mission to fulfil, and God, our Creator, will provide the power I need to fulfil it.

After pawning my watch one Saturday in order to pay a bill, I heard the sound of a car horn as a Rastaman yelled, "Vander!" It was Lenny, a great percussionist. "Wally would like to see you," he said. "I'd like to see him as well," I replied. Some days later Wally called me, and I then went to meet him in temporary accommodation, as he was visiting London from Guyana, where he now resides.

I was impressed by his huge catalogue, and massive contribution to reggae music. We reminisced and got up to date with where we were in our lives.

I gave him a copy of my album, which he said he'd listen to with his brother Charlie. Charlie was looking after the business in England, while he took care of things in Guyana, with a first-class recording studio. He wasn't staying long, but said he'd be back soon, and would listen to my album in my absence, as he didn't want our friendship to cloud his judgement. I agreed.

It was a sad time, as Wally visited Gregory Isaacs' sickbed almost every day in Harrow. The last time I saw Gregory Isaacs, he was standing outside Wally's house, as I was on my way somewhere, in the grip of drug and alcohol addiction. I quietly hailed him, and he responded from a short distance, as I hurried to get to my crack pipe and alcohol. That's how I remember him. I often sang Gregory Isaacs' songs when high on crack, cocaine and alcohol. I sang through the void and the pain, with songs like 'Beach Party', 'She May Not Be in the Top Ten', 'Bits and Pieces' and 'Lovely Lady', and I identified with him as a fellow crack smoker who couldn't and wouldn't stop on a permanent basis. I sang his songs in the crack houses, on the streets, on the buses and on the trains. I felt what he was feeling, I felt his joy and pain in his songs.

It was of no surprise to me when Wally spoke of Gregory's painful passing with cancer. I didn't ask him about his opinion on my album, but allowed him space to grieve, along with millions of people around the world who had heard the news. 'Danger in Your Eyes' came into my head. I remembered rocking to that Gregory Isaacs' tune as it was being played by the mighty Sir Coxon Sound, at a boat dance on the River Thames. With ganja smoking and champagne flowing, and everyone dressed for the occasion, the women looked like they'd stepped out of Vogue magazine, and the men from Savile Row.

When the captain decided to turn around and head to port, we were in no mood to stop the party, as a group of us offered to pay him to carry on sailing. "It's not worth my license, much as I would like to," he said. I refer to those days as the roaring twenties, the days before crack, cocaine and alcohol turned day into night.

Wally had been in the dark concerning Gregory's grave condition. Apparently, Gregory knew he had just a few weeks left on this side of life but didn't burden anyone with it. I understand that he refused medication, didn't cry through the pain, and passed away with dignity, while resting.

Wally had hoped he'd recover. I'd known differently, but kept it to myself, hoping I was wrong. Thank you, Gregory Isaacs, for the joy and inspiration you gave me, from boyhood to manhood.

On another visit to Wally, he told me that Charlie liked my album and thought it was commercially viable. He had yet to hear it himself but was already swayed by Charlie's verdict. He also expressed a liking for my documentary about Samuel Ajai Crowther, the slave boy who became a bishop, and invited me to tour the schools in Guyana, giving lectures on the subject. I accepted his offer.

As life unfolded, I was admitted for a hernia operation at the Whittington Hospital, where I'd worked on Radio LNR. It felt strange being a patient instead. Andrew, a Jehovah Witness and a brother with whom I had bible discussions every Sunday, came to give me a lift home soon after I came around.

I got myself a walking stick, and soon discovered the disadvantages of living on my own and being without a girlfriend. Cooking and cleaning became more difficult. Everything slowed down, as I limited my exertions, in order to recover. Wally had to return to his family and business without me. I was still using the stick and it was considered unwise to travel to Guyana in that condition.

Before he left, he was visited by Jah Shaka, whom I hadn't seen for many years. Jah Shaka and I had a history that took us back to a time when we shared a prison cell in Ashford Remand Centre as teenagers. He had his sound system even then and played out even if it meant hauling huge speaker boxes up the road on foot. Yes! That's how the mighty Jah Shaka, the spiritual dub warrior sound started. I was glad to see and hear of his international success. He had referred to me as Nat King Cole, and I was encouraged by that, as Wally's interest grew in my album.

Wally left and returned with Shelley G, Soca Queen of Guyana 2010. She sang as sweet as a bird and was making the crossover into reggae music with his help. I attended two radio interviews that I had arranged at Omega Radio 104.2 FM, promoting her album launch at Bar SE19, a lovely restaurant in Norwood, South London. The album is entitled 'Conflict'. The launch was a great success, and I was glad to share the company of Tappa Zukie, Big Youth, Elroy 'Bassie' from Black Slate and Scorpion, a childhood friend, whose family is strongly connected with the music business. It was good to talk to Castro Brown, a man who'd raised the profile of reggae music in this country, with the great Dennis Brown and other artists.

I was honoured to have met Dennis at his family home in England many years ago as well as later in life. With brother Asher, I helped out filming on stage with a camcorder. I hadn't seen him for many years. Drug and alcohol addiction had held me prisoner and cut me off from so many people. Now I was enjoying my freedom. At another meeting, Wally said he liked my album, although it needed mixing and mastering, and he had decided to include it in his Vizion Sounds Catalogue. I was grateful for his involvement, as all tracks and songs were registered and coded by Charlie, his brother. This also included an album of music to poetry I'd produced, entitled 'GTMI in Motion'. GTMI is the Amharic word for poetry or poems and is equal to number seven. It was

Wally who inspired me to seek an Amharic name for that album.

I explained to Wally that my album title 'Every Heartbeat', was a reference to my journey through drug and alcohol addiction. He felt there was something missing in the album, apart from mixing and mastering, and I felt it too, but couldn't figure it out at the time. It wasn't just a matter of adding five more tracks.

I was in a meeting with Wally one day, as he answered a call from Guyana. At the end of the phone call he said his son's mother came up with the solution of a narration before each track. I said, "That's it, I'll see to it straight away." So off I went, wrote the narrations and recorded them within a fortnight and footed the bill with my money. Charlie played the narration while we listened. From the very first track, it was unanimously agreed that we'd found the missing ingredient to the album. Wally left with Asher and Shelley G soon after that, to spend more time in Guyana.

A month or so later, I received a phone call from Wally suggesting I make a change and call my album 'From Rehab to Life'. I agreed at once. It fit the album like a glove. On his return with Shelley G, I received a copy of the album with the narrations. I was on a cloud as I listened to 'From Rehab to Life' and thanked Wally, Charlie, Asher and all the staff at Vizion Sounds Records.

Wally sent my album to Transition Mastering Studios in South London, and with Jason at the controls, it returned even better. I didn't give Wally the files to any of my tracks for remixing and, as a result, my album was cheaply and superficially remastered with three other albums from various artists in a package deal of one thousand pounds, and for which I'm grateful. I thanked God, Wally, Asher, Charlie and all Vizion Sound staff again. I thought the CD cover deserved to be nominated for an award when I saw it for the first time. It was created and designed by Ray Hayden and his company Opaz, who were once based in Hackney, close to the Hackney Empire, but was now relocated to St John's Wood. In all fairness, Charlie also had some input in the design, myself included.

The idea of an autobiography for the album came up. It would be in both book and audio form. Preliminary arrangements for a music video documentary were assigned to Andrew Fraser, Charlie Fraser's son, and director of 'Youth Skills Network', 'Toolbox Media' and 'UR Brand'. Charlie Fraser is the dad that a lot of children would like to have, and many women would love as a husband. Furthermore, he's a loving and caring son to his elderly mother, a true brother to Wally, supportive to all his family and friends, and easy going with everyone. His pleasures are Jazz, photography, drinking and golf as well as caring for a lot of people.

I was in Tottenham one day when by chance I met Pongo, a friend I hadn't seen for twenty years. I gave him a promotional copy of my album to let him know where I was at. He in turn gave me a flyer that introduced me to his club, Charlie Wright's International in Pitfield Street, Hoxton. He invited me to showcase my songs there and to come and look at the place. I readily agreed, as he continued his journey with a friend in the opposite direction. I told Wally about the meeting with Pongo, and we decided that we would go with Charlie, to see the place, with a view to promoting live reggae acts at the venue.

Suddenly, showcasing my songs evolved into showcasing reggae music, and a chance for the music industry to showcase their artists, and find new talent as well. The club came fully equipped with a stage, two sets of drums, piano, PA system and a sound engineer. There's security, a DJ booth, an Italian diner, all in a club internationally known for jazz acts.

We planned to change the cuisine to West Indian on Reggae nights, to be held on the first and last Friday of each month. We decided to start with Lovers Rock. Carol Thompson was booked to appear with Shelley G in support, and with Shelley G as the headline act the following Friday. Shelley G gave a fine show and Carol Thompson was sensational on Friday, November 30, 2012. I was MC (Master of Ceremonies) for the show, with Natty B from Choice FM as DJ. The crowd wasn't as big as expected; nonetheless, it was a happy occasion. Everyone had a good time up close and personal with the artists on stage, singing and dancing. I thought about doing an a cappella rendition of 'Love on the Internet' as MC on the night but let go of the idea.

One Sunday afternoon, just before all this happened, I visited Pentonville Prison and chaired a speech on recovery from drugs and alcohol. It was a privilege and an honour to be of some assistance to these inmates on their journey to freedom from drugs and alcohol addiction, which to them is a prison within the prison. They helped keep my memory fresh as to where I'd been, and where I am now. As an ex-con, it's a miraculous experience, entering and leaving a jail the same day, on behalf of recovery and the Fellowships for drug addicts and alcoholics.

Prison officers from HMP Belmarsh, Wormwood Scrubs and Wandsworth have made me tea as a guest of the institution. I had never imagined that this would happen in a million years. Such is the power of God, our ultimate authority in recovery. God be with you all!

"From Rehab to Life is my biggest project!" Wally exclaimed. "There's a buzz that's building around it, and a lot of people would like to get involved." I welcomed the news as I added the interest I'd found, coming from so many agencies who had said that 'From Rehab to Life' was inspirational. They were willing to explore ways of sponsorship that included a financial package, built around my life as an artist, and the project, 'From Rehab to Life.'

I returned to see him some days later, on a 106 bus. Suddenly, everything went quiet, as the bus ride came to a premature end by Clapton Square, en route to Whitechapel. There were no moving vehicles up ahead, going in either direction, as traffic from behind also gradually came to a standstill. The pavements were deserted, the shops closed, and an eerie blanket of silence enveloped me as I stepped off the bus. The driver gave no explanation for the abrupt halt to our journey. The few people on the streets appeared to be heading for refuge.

As I continued my journey on foot, I saw a dozen or more policemen, equipped with riot gear, standing on the Narrow Way, opposite Clarence Road. The air was suddenly filled with rocks and glass bottle missiles raining down on the policemen, as I walked towards them. I didn't stop to ask any questions but passed through the men in blue. It seemed as though the police were on a peace protest, as they made no attempt to advance against the angry and hostile group of young men on Clarence Road.

Still oblivious to the cause of the situation, I eventually arrived at the house. By then, the sound of the TV was drowned out by the noise of helicopters circling above, with their blades menacingly chopping the air, to the heavy sound of the engines. The atmosphere was such, that one expected to see armoured vehicles and soldiers on the streets at any moment. But it didn't happen.

I returned to my home by train. The cause of the situation only came to light the next day. East, West, North and South London had reacted with looting, arson, criminal damage, attacks on the constabulary and members of the public, after the police shot dead Mark Duggan, a young gangster from Tottenham, on the 5th August, 2011.

No longer involved in gangster activities, I was distributing albums including Gregory Isaacs' 'Substance Free', Luciano's 'Gideon', and 'Musicology' by Big Youth, to the small number of surviving record shops in London, on behalf of Wally's Vizion Sounds Records.

I've noticed there's a strong demand for vinyl and second-hand records, which appear to be doing better than new CD sales. Isn't that telling us something about what's missing in a lot of music today? And that is love, an ingredient we all need.

Wally told me the story behind Gregory's 'Substance Free'. Apparently, he asked Gregory to abstain from the crack pipe before each session. Gregory stuck to the agreement, hence the title 'Substance Free'. And that was a man who thought it was impossible to give up crack.

I always thought it was possible to abstain from drugs and alcohol but didn't realise what a monumental task it was. It was easy to stop for a time, but to stay clean indefinitely is a miracle and a gift from God, whether you believe in our Creator or not. The rain falls and sun shines on everyone, and recovery is there for everyone, whether they believe in God or not.

Over fourtenn years ago, I received a letter that said, "Dear Vander Peter, Alcoholics Anonymous invites you to a reception at The Houses of Parliament on the seventeenth of March 2005, at four thirty p.m. It will be hosted by Mr Tony Coleman, MP for Putney. It will take place in the Atlee Room, Portcullis House, Westminster. Portcullis House is the new building across the road from Big Ben, which serves as an extension to the Palace of Westminster. Mr Coleman will open the reception. Two AA members will then describe AA history, and current work. This will be followed by two other AA's sharing their experiences of drinking problems and subsequent recovery. There will also be brief presentations by three professionals working in the field of alcoholism and addiction, who have experience of working with AA."

I was invited to share my experiences of drinking difficulties and subsequent recovery, for twenty minutes. Members of the House of Lords and the House of Commons were in attendance. Also present were doctors, psychiatrists and other professionals in the field of addiction. My speech was not prepared and was well received by an attentive audience.

During light refreshments after my speech, I was invited to the launch of a new rehab called 'Success in Recovery'. They were based in Kent, and the launch, which I attended, took place in a boat on the River Thames. I spoke to psychiatrists and counsellors, exploring ways in which we could work together for the common good. There I was drinking fruit juice with canapés, whilst others were indulging in red and white wine. That experience in itself was a miracle.

I spoke to Lesley Reardon, the director who invited me to the event. She said she'd call me to arrange my visit to the rehab, as soon as she found the best way to incorporate my skills and experience with the other professionals working there. After speaking to her several times on the phone, when she said that she was extremely busy, I'm still open to that invitation, fourteen years later and ongoing.

I recently attended a blue plaque unveiling ceremony in honour of Liz Mitchell, lead singer of Bony M, at her childhood family home in Harlesden. Her father Mr Norman Mitchell MBE, awarded for his services in the community, was also honoured at the occasion, and is still very active in the community at the grand age of ninety-three.

The ceremony was presented by The Federation Of Reggae Music (FORM-UK), and Brent Council Reggae Focus Sounds of Jamaica, in recognition of her mighty achievements with Bony M. Delroy Washington, a UK reggae veteran, founder member, and CEO of FORM-UK, introduced the proceedings. Other speakers that followed were: Bobby Thomas, the Mayor of Brent and a former athlete; councillor Lincoln Beswick, MBE and project champion of Brent Council; followed by Winston Francis, a FORM-UK executive member and a legendary reggae singer-songwriter.

Liz Mitchell, the woman of the moment, spoke of her gratitude, her good fortune, and the honour that was bestowed upon her by her fans and the music business. Norman Mitchell wrapped things up with a powerful and inspirational speech that transported us back to the days when things were a lot more hostile for black people in the UK. He'd been recently knocked down by a car but made a swift and miraculous recovery. He stood firm and upright on his feet, with eyes that haven't dimmed, and with a steady voice that uttered words of wisdom. I felt honoured to have been invited. The committee had taken the view that the time had arrived to award Blue Plaques to the living as well as to the dearly departed. I totally agreed!

The Moringa tree has also been a great discovery, although its therapeutic and preventative uses regarding our health have been known for thousands of years. Why was this knowledge hidden? Moringa has helped me in ways that doctors and pharmaceutical drugs were unable to do. It is also the world's number one food supplement. It actually strengthens the immune system and helps in the treatment and prevention of over three hundred diseases and works alongside pharmaceutical drugs. The seeds of the Moringa tree, purify and clarify undrinkable water. Known as the Miracle Tree as well as the Tree of Life, it is referred to in the Bible in Exodus, Chapter XV, Verse XXV, as the branches that turned the bitter waters sweet for Moses and the Children of Israel, at a place called Mara.

It has erased the increasing pain and discomfort that dug into my hamstrings and the right side of my waist for over eighteen months. Blood tests revealed nothing, and physiotherapy proved ineffective. It has also alleviated my piles, improved my eyesight, and given me more energy, mental balance and clarity. It's a great aphrodisiac and good for reproductive health, has anti-ageing powers, and has been used in beauty products for decades. I love Moringa! Thank you, God!

Leah recently revealed to me that their mother often took her and Nathan to the crack house with her. She would leave them in a room with other people's children while she indulged in her habit. My shock, horror and anger lasted a split second, as they served no useful purpose. I refuse to hold on to these self-destructive traits today. Instead, I thank God for bringing Nathan and Leah through these traumatic experiences. Michelle was no longer here for me to question her about it. She always saw herself as a good mother and wondered why everyone else was complaining. Such is the fatal nature of the disease of addiction. Nathan and Leah are doing well, considering the hell that they've been through, which also includes many scenes of violent abuse against their mother. They loved her, and they love her now, such is the power of unconditional love.

I was invited to attend a meeting called Family and Friends, as a guest speaker by Karen Wright, who runs the fellowship. She was concerned that their much-needed organisation was about to lose government funding. It's for families and friends affected by drug and alcohol addiction.

The spiritual, mental and physical devastation was apparent. Some of these women had suffered strokes, heart attacks, depression, high blood pressure, and were living in constant fear in co-dependent relationships. I heard the pain and despair in their voices and saw it in their body language.

So, it was good to hear that some of them were ready to let go of their sick partners at long last.

Most of all, I was glad to hear of their triumphs over adversity. I was moved by an addict mother's story, in the company of her adult daughter. Her daughter had been supportive through all the pain, fear and destruction of her addiction as well as in recovery. It reminded me of the many times Nathan and Leah said they used to creep into their mother's bedroom, just to reassure themselves that she was still alive.

Another lady, who sat close to me, said she could hit me with a stick after hearing about my achievements in the last nine years. She questioned how much more I could've achieved, had I not served the insanity of drug and alcohol addiction for so long. I then told her that I had been enriched, strengthened, and empowered by my experiences. I also told her that spiritual progress and growth in my recovery had helped me shed shame, anger, regret, resentment, remorse and irresponsibility. As a result, I had acquired the tools to help myself, and others, under the aegis of 'From Rehab to Life', with God's grace.

Chapter 29
Revelations

As I fast forward into what was the present moment, I felt ill at ease, perturbed by the serious lack of investment and doubtful of Wally's sincerity, motive and integrity after approximately two and a half years of no progress, I began to acknowledge the truth. I questioned his compatibility with my project that included my two albums of songs and poetry, a drama documentary and two or three radio programmes that I had produced and presented and financed many years before he came along. I had entrusted copies of my labour of love in his care with a view to potentially do business with. I confided with my soul father, Father Mikael, a founder member and former priest in charge of The Ethiopian Orthodox Tewahedo Church of Saint Mary Tsion. As soon as I made mention of Wally's character, history and practices, my soul father looked at me straight in the eyes and strongly advised me to cut off all connections with him immediately, in order to avoid the unseen and disastrous consequences to my lifetime project.

I spoke to Wally at the earliest opportunity and made it crystal clear that any potential agreement that I had discussed with him was no longer valid as I found it impossible to proceed any further with him and my project under any circumstances. He asked me about royalty payments. I responded by saying that his contribution didn't warrant royalties and I'd repay him the little he'd spent with interest as soon as any money was made and there were others who'd spent a lot more than him and expected nothing in return, although I intended to reward them out of my deepest appreciation for helping me to lay down the foundations for my work when others had no faith in me and many years before he came on the scene. "Are we still friends?" he asked.

"Yes!" I exclaimed, and no more was said.

A few years after that conversation, I asked a brother to check on the registration of my two albums with PRS.

It was a bombshell to discover that Wally with the help of his brother Charlie had claimed fifty to one hundred percent royalties for my tracks. My gut feeling and Father Tesfa Mikael's advice was right. As a result, I'm now going through the painful process of re-establishing my full rights to my lifetime work and ambition borne out of my decades of suffering and the need to help others avoid, or ascend from the same or similar dire conditions, from which I was miraculously set free by The Grace of The Most High!

Me with my first child and son, JaJa

From left to right: Vander Pierre, Nathan Pierre, and Leah Pierre.

Mr grandsons, Isaiah Pierre (left) and Malachi Pierre (right).

My twin daughters, Makeda Pierre (left) and Naomi Pierre
(right).

From left to right: Nathan Pierre, Glen Pierre, Curtis Pierre, Malachi Pierre, Nathaniel Pierre, Immanuel Pierre, and Isaiah Pierre.

From left to right: Israel McLeod, Leah Pierre, Jayson McLeod.

My granddaughter Eleri from my son JaJa.

At the Xgangsters Odyssey album launch in London September 2018.

As Captain Morano, leader of modern-day London pirates,
in the film *Polly II*.

IV Appendix:

Caribbean Odysseys

C.1775 B.C.: Siboney moving through, the Southern Caribbean. In Arawak, the word Siboney means 'stone people'.1st century A.D: Arawak moving from South America through the Caribbean.

C.1200 A.D.: Caribs moving through the Islands.

October 12, 1492: Christopher Columbus lands in San Salvador (Guanahani) in the Bahamas. November 3, 1493: Columbus discovers and names Dominica.

Columbus names Monserrat after the monastery in Catalonia where the Jesuits began.

Columbus names Antigua (Yarumaqui or Waladli) after the church of Santa Marta La Antigua in Seville.

Columbus names St Christopher (later St Kitts) after his sainted namesake.

Bull of Partition: on the urging of Ferdinand & Isabella of Spain, pope Alexander VI assigns the West Indies to that country.

1494: Columbus discovers Xaymaca or Jamaica, the Arawak word for 'well-watered'.

1498: Columbus discovers and names St Vincent.

Columbus discovers and names Trinidad (Trinidado because of the Holy Trinity and the fact that this was his third voyage).

1502: Columbus discovers and names St Lucia (Hewannora).

1508: Sebastian de Ocampo learns that Cuba is a very large island. His proof? Circumnavigation.

1510: Diego Velasquez lands at Guantanamo Bay to colonise Cuba for Spain.

1536: The Portuguese visit and name Los Barbudos (Barbados) after the bearded fig tree they found there.

1542: Bartolomeo de las Casas writes 'A Short Account of the Destruction of the Indies'.

1563: Hawkins begins slaving between Sierra Leone and Hispaniola.

1595: Sir Robert Dudley visits Trinidad and Ralegh sacks San Josef on that island. Ralegh sails for the South American mainland and gives an account of it in his 'Discoverie of Guiana'.

1605: Captain Cataline claims Barbados for Britain.

1609: Robert Harcourt claims Guiana for Britain.

1620: The Dutch establish Essequibo and Demerara. (When Dutch Guiana came into being it was known as Surinam).

1623: St Christopher, later St Kitts, is the first English settlement in the Caribbean.

1632: Antigua is settled by the English, under Edward Warner, the first governor of the island.

1634: The Dutch take possession of Curacao.

1635: The French colonise Martinique and Guadeloupe.

1639: Parliament set up in the British possession of Barbados.

1649–1685: Irish, Scots, Welsh and English prisoners dispatched as slaves or indentured labour to Barbados and Monserrat.

1655: The English seize Jamaica from the Spanish. Black slaves escape to the mountains. These runaways, known as Maroons, lead a separate guerrilla existence for more than 200 years.

1671: Morgan sacks Panama and returns to Jamaica.

1675: The Caribs of St Vincent take in negro slaves who had been shipwrecked on neighbouring Bequia. A mixed people, known as Black Caribs, are the result.

1692: Port Royal, the buccaneer haven in Jamaica, is destroyed by earthquake.

1702: The British take possession of St Kitts.

1705: The last Carib raid on Antigua.

1748: The Caribs hold Dominica. The island is declared neutral territory by the Treaty of Aix La Chapelle. There is still a Carib quarter today.

1749: The Dutch sign a treaty with the Bush Negroes in Surinam. The Bush Negroes were descended from runaway slaves.

1756: The English conquer Dominica.

1762: Rodney and Monckton secure St Lucia for the English, this would be disputed by the French until 1796, when it became an English colony.

1763: Josephine, future Empress and wife to Napoleon, is born in Trois Islets, Martinique.

1782: Admiral Rodney saves the British West Indies from the French at the Battle of the Saints (The French call this the Battle of Dominica).

1783: The first year of carnival in Port of Spain, Trinidad.

1784–1787: Nelson is in the West Indies. He spends much time at English Harbour, Antigua, and in St Kitts, where he marries Fanny Nisbet.

1795: Britain puts down slave and Carib uprisings in St Vincent and Grenada. Caribs and the so-called Black Caribs are transported to the island of Ruatan in the Bay Islands of Honduras. Their English-speaking descendants still live in the Islas De La Bahia and along the north coast of Honduras and Belize, where they are known as Garifunas.

1797: St John's, the capital of Antigua, is destroyed by fire. The English take Trinidad from Spain.

1801: Toussaint L'Ouverture declares Haiti independent of France and appoints himself president for life. He is the first black head of state in the Caribbean. He is overthrown in 1802 and dies in a French prison the following year.

1807: Britain abolishes slave trading.

1833: Britain abolishes slavery by an Act of Parliament. Immigrants from India, Mauritius, Syria, Lebanon and the Far East bolster the work force in Trinidad, British Guiana and Jamaica.

1838: Slaves freed in the British Islands.

1841: St John's in Antigua destroyed by fire again.

1847: Slavery ended in the Danish islands.

1848: The French end slavery.

1865: End of the American Civil War. Slavery eradicated from America.

Morant Bay Rebellion in Jamaica over worsening economic conditions.

1872: Kingston replaces Spanish Town as the capital of Jamaica.

1873: Slavery ended in the Dutch colonies.

Slavery ended in Puerto Rico, a Spanish possession.

1880-1884: Serious disturbances at carnival in Trinidad. Stick dancing and men dressing as women forbidden by police.

1886: Slavery ended in the Spanish island of Cuba.

Further influx of Indian, Chinese, Maltese and Madeiran labour.

1898: The Spanish American War in Cuba. Spain obliged to make Cuba independent and to cede Puerto Rico to the US.

1902: Mont Pele erupts in Martinique and destroys the old capital of St Pierre. Within five minutes, more than 30,000 people die.

Soufriere erupts in St Vincent, killing most of the Carib population.

1910: Flotation of Trinidad Oilfields Inc.

1912: Mamie born.

In June, Lovey's Trinidad String Band record 'Trinidad–Paseo', known in English as 'See What You Do'. This is the first calypso recording to see the light of day.

1915: The British West India Regiment goes to the Great War in Europe.

1915–1924: US occupation of the Dominican Republic.

1915–1933: US occupation of Haiti.

1917: US purchases some of the Virgin Islands, including St Thomas, from Denmark.

1935: My mother, Jean, is born in St John's, Antigua, on the 31st May.

1935–1938: Labour disputes and strikes in the British Caribbean. Beginning of the Federation Movement and the rise of Nationalism.

1945: On February 6, Robert Nesta Marley is born in Nine Miles, St Ann, Jamaica.

1948: Castries, the capital of St Lucia, is destroyed by fire.

On June 22, the S.S. Empire Windrush docks at Tilbury, carrying 493 passengers from Jamaica including the Calypsonians Lord Kitchener, Lord Beginner, Lord Woodbine and Mona Baptise. This is the first large group of West Indian immigrants to enter the UK after World War Two.

1951: Castries in St Lucia is burnt down again.

1958: Federation of the West Indies inaugurated in the British Islands.

Cuban Revolution: Fidel Castro overthrows the US backed dictator, Batista.

1962: In February, Robert Marley, supported by the Beverly All Stars, makes his debut, recording on Federal with 'Judge Not'. Lesley Kong produces.

The Federation collapses. Jamaica and Trinidad secure their independence.

1963: Enoch Powell is Minister of Health in the UK. He brings trained doctors from India and Pakistan. West Indian nurses continue to be in demand.

: London Transport has recruitment office in Barbados.

1966: Barbados gains independence

: Br. Guiana gains independence.

1967: St Lucia gains independence.

1970: Guiana becomes Republic of Guyana.

1974: Grenada gains independence.

1978: Dominica gains independence.

1979: Eugenia Charles, in Dominica, is the first woman to head a Caribbean government.

St Vincent gains independence.

1981: Antigua gains independence.

Author's Note

If you wish to support the aim of From Rehab to Life Foundation in any way, please go to From Rehab to Life Foundation aka fromrehabtolifefoundation.org, or download our album *XGangsters Odyssey*, or the single "A Martyr for Ganja".

All proceeds go to "From Rehab to Life Foundation" aka fromrehabtolifefoundation.org, which helps to steer the young away from drug and alcohol addiction, violence and crime. Please share this with others. We also have another album entitled *From Rehab to Life* awaiting release to support the same goal as this book.

Wishing everyone love, good health and happiness.

Tamara Gabriel